AMERICA

PublishAmerica
Baltimore

First printing

ISBN: 1-4137-2564-3
PUBLISHED BY PUBLISHAMERICA, LLLP
www.publishamerica.com
Baltimore

Printed in the United States of America

This book is dedicated to
Catherine and Kimmy,
two beautiful souls
who know the true meaning
of
unconditional love.

Introduction

Up until last night I had the introduction to this book all nicely written and had been quite happy with it, too…and then I sat down and watched a documentary about a young girl with anorexia nervosa on the TV. I didn't expect too much from the programme at first, as I usually discover that documentaries about eating disorders only seem to skim the surface of the REAL problems involved. I may not be an expert on much in life, but, having had one eating disorder or another for all of my adult life, I can claim to know a little of what I am talking about here! However, my reaction after watching this programme really surprised me, and warranted scrapping the first introduction and starting all over again! Not something I like to do either, being somewhat of a lapsed perfectionist!

I went to bed soon after the programme ended and simply couldn't sleep for the anger I felt welling up inside me. Anger that nobody seemed to be asking this girl how *she* felt; how everyone just seemed to be focusing on the food issues and not the underlying reasons for her illness; that nobody just held her close and told her how much they loved her and how very special she was. Of course, they may have done that off camera, but I wanted her parents to do it there and then, to show other parents, other caring people, that love and affection and validation was as much a part of recovery as feeding tubes (yuk) and calorie charts.

This particular anorexic girl's illness followed a familiar pattern and was all too similar to my own story—she went through periods of losing dramatic amounts of weight, being hospitalised, gaining enough weight to satisfy the doctors so they would allow her to go home, and then losing it all again. When she was back at home, her parents watched her eating her meals like a hawk; they seemed to measure their approval for her by how many potatoes she ate that meal, or how much cereal she poured out for herself, when it was obvious to me that her very soul was crying out for love and attention.

There was even a psychiatrist on the programme who had the audacity to say;

"Well, of course, we really don't know how anorexics FEEL when they eat…" and I wanted to scream at the TV;

"ASK THEM THEN!!!!!!" and in fact my 12 year old daughter picked up on that very omission and said the words for me. How could SHE see that blindingly obvious fact and not some eminent psychiatrist? God, it made me so mad!!

You see, it's not about food at all. Oh yes, food disturbance is the symptom that shows and is the symptom that must be treated when life is threatened, but there is so much more to it than that. I didn't realise that myself for years, and I kept on trying to solve my eating problems when there was an absolute maelstrom of feelings swirling around underneath. The thing is, I couldn't say at the time what those feelings were, but now I CAN. And this is the main reason I have written this book…

When you are in the grip of anorexia, bulimia or compulsive overeating, you aren't always able to put words to your feelings and emotions as they are so powerful and all consuming that you turn to the food in order to take away the pain of those feelings. It took me years before I could acknowledge the tremendous fear that I lived with day after day; the anger, the guilt, the deep pain and sadness, the feelings of rejection and being so unworthy that I shouldn't even inhabit my space on this earth. I lived with those feelings for as long as I can remember, from being a small child, but I had no words for them, and food was my comfort, my control in this crazy and hurtful world, and my one true friend that never went away.

That sounds dramatic, but eating disorders ARE dramatic. They are life threatening. Twenty percent of all anorexics die. It is an incredibly sad fact. And the ones who live on go through absolute hell on earth. The bulimics go through another kind of torture again, and the compulsive eaters live with self-hate and self-disgust every day of their lives. It is no way to live. It is no way to BE. As a people we need to change our attitudes towards our children, so that they grow up with a healthy self-esteem and never need to grasp desperately onto eating disorders or any other kinds of addiction to find their validation or their escape. We are obsessed these days with material possessions, with monetary gain, with stature in society—what we DO has become so much more important than who we ARE. And all the while we ignore the human beings inside the suits or the uniforms we wear. We tend to give children our love and attention more because they do well in exams or acquire a prestigious job than because of the wonderful people that they are. We are sowing the seeds for poor self-worth and terribly low self-esteem on a mass scale when we live this way. There then follows a need to reach out for external comfort, whether it be in food, alcohol, gambling, whatever …all these addictions have a very similar root cause

This book is MY voice. I don't speak for anyone other than myself, but this is what eating disorders were like for ME. This is where MY eating problems came from and how they progressed and what lay beneath them, and maybe my words will strike a chord in the hearts of other sufferers who have not found their voice yet. Maybe my words will help someone who is close to a person with an eating disorder to see them from a different point of view and be able to help them more. Maybe my words will stop another professional saying;

"Of course, we don't know how they FEEL."

This is how I felt. It may be how other people in similar positions feel too, it may not be, but at least it can be a starting point for discussion; i.e., Is THIS how you feel? Have you ever felt pain like THIS?

We need to talk to our children more, we need to see who they are, we need to look at ALL they are, not just the academic side of them or the parts that achieve, but every little quirk of their personality and we need to love them all unconditionally. We need to nurture them, protect them when needs be, tell them how special they are and make them feel like when the time comes, their wings are strong enough to take them out into the world and allow them to follow their dreams.

That kind of love is food for the soul—I wish to God I had had that when I was growing up, and then I wouldn't have been left with this gaping hole inside that I can never seem to fill. Maybe…just maybe, writing this book will help to do just that, and will tie up some loose ends for me, and hopefully for you as well. If you are going through an eating disorder right now, my heart is with you and you are not alone. You CAN get through this, you really can, and there is untold happiness on the other side, but there is also a whole lot of crap to get through along the way!!!! It is worth it though, it really is. Keep going, hold your head up high and know that you ARE so very worthy of your place on this earth. Nobody else can be a better YOU than YOU, and never ever forget that……

Chapter One
Sowing the Seeds

The events that are about to follow in this book are true and make up the fabric of my weird and wonderful life. They may not have happened at the exact time that I have said they did, mainly because my memory for dates isn't THAT good, but my memory for feelings and situations is as clear as ever. Yes, there is a little bit of dramatic license here and there, but only to make the story a little more readable and a little less vague; the essence of it all is true. I have changed the names of many of the people involved and I dare say there are people in my life who will come and tell me that 'this bit isn't true' and so on. But, do you know what?? I don't care!! This story is bigger than mere facts and needs telling in all its glory—or otherwise!! The incredibly severe diet which led to my anorexia, then to bulimia, then to compulsive overeating and depression, and my many other self-destructive habits began on February 23 1978; that date will be etched in my mind forever. But the seeds that flourished inside me and made this whole crazy lifetime possible were planted a long time before that, from birth even. An eating disorder certainly doesn't just appear overnight, and neither will it disappear without a whole lot of love and nurturing.

Anyway…here goes, here is MY story…GULP!!

The Baby Cries…

The baby's weakening cries can be heard right across the park that night, but they largely go ignored by the inhabitants of this small cluster of caravans. It has been heard so many times before after all—always on an evening; always after the young Canadian comes back from whatever he does during the day. No one seems to know where he goes or what he does, but it obviously can't pay very well or else no way would he and his pitiful family be living in this run-down caravan park, usually reserved for those that have nowhere better to go…

It's exactly the same pattern every night—the baby starts to cry—she's only little, maybe six or seven months old, and she's probably only crying for her food like all babies do. She certainly doesn't cry any more than any other infant, but maybe the young Canadian doesn't know that. Neither does his wife, it seems, for her voice is often raised in anger at the baby as well, but it is always the father who ends up pushing the pram outside. He opens the door, and takes the pram, with the screaming baby still inside, as far from the caravan as he can go before he reaches the perimeter fence. His dark face is contorted with rage. He looks as if he would gladly push the pram to the ends of the earth if it meant he could be rid of his daughter for good. The rusty and broken perimeter fence is never far enough away for him.

It is pitch black outside at this time of night and there are no streetlights to brighten up the park. The wind is bitingly cold and the young Canadian huddles up inside his jacket as he puts the brake on the pram and walks away. If you crept up to peek inside the pram right there and then, you would see a tiny red face, eyes all screwed up, fists tight with rage. Her little body is moving furiously beneath the faded covers. Her hands would be freezing cold to the touch and her cries would grow hoarser by the minute as her strength ebbs away. Eventually she will give up her crying; no one will come, they never do.

Is she frightened as she opens her eyes for a moment and sees nothing but a sheet of blackness in front of her? Does she realise that she is all alone? What does she think and feel as she lies there for an hour, sometimes more, usually falling asleep at last, despite the constant gnawing in her stomach? Has she already become resigned to her cries going unanswered? Does she know that she will never come first in the lives of her young and incapable parents? Have the seeds already been sown; the seeds that will give her a lifetime of vulnerability, neediness, and fear? Will she close her eyes each night of her life thereafter and feel the darkness enfolding her, the never-ending darkness with its unknown fears? I wonder…

I can hear the raised voices, the crying of the mother as she weeps in the utter despair of her miserable existence. I can hear the hysterical voice of the young Canadian as he fights to maintain his number one ranking in this wretched family. He refuses to be ousted by a needy baby—no way. I can hear that baby's cries, I feel the cold on her fingers and I can see the blackness that covers her tiny world. I feel the hunger, I sense the fear…it is all mine…

For that baby was me…and I am her…and this is my life…

Four Years Old...

I am four years old and I am waiting quietly in a huge long corridor that never seems to end in a big brown building in the middle of the town. Nanna and Granpa sit on either side of me and nobody speaks. I have no idea what we are waiting for but I get the feeling that it is very important and that I should be very good. Nanna and Granpa both look very serious and when they talk to each other, they do it very quietly and with their faces turned away from me so that I can't see. It is a bit scary. I wish I knew what was happening.

A lady comes out of a brown door opposite us and asks us to follow her and we all go into an enormous room where we are told to sit down in front of a huge desk. There is a man sitting behind it, wearing glasses and looking very cross. Why is everyone so frowny today?

I sit there, feeling smaller and smaller all the time, and wonder if people have forgotten I am there, but then I hear my name being spoken by the man, except he isn't saying it right. He is calling me Sylvia Anne R. and that isn't me anymore. That is the me that I was when I was a baby but now I'm Anne H. and that is something completely different. I don't like being called Sylvia. It isn't me at all. It is my Mummy's name and I hate it.

And then before we know it, we have to go back outside again and whatever has happened is all over. I look up at Granpa and he tells me that I have just been adopted. What does that mean, I want to know? It means that you are ours now, he tells me. You are our child, and you are going to live with us till you are grown up. And then we go home.

******

I still don't really understand what 'adopted' means as I have always lived with Nanna and Granpa. I can't remember ever being with anyone else and I just thought I would always live with them anyway. I didn't know I had to be 'adopted' to be allowed to live with them. I know I have a Mummy, who lives with my two little sisters, Gayle and Diane, but I don't think I ever had a Daddy. Nobody ever talks about one anyway.

Maybe now Nanna and Granpa are my Mummy and Daddy. I ask them because I would love to have someone to call Mummy and Daddy, but they say No. Everyone is still the same as they used to be. Nothing will change. I still call Nanna and Granpa 'Nanna and Granpa', and I still call my Mummy 'Mummy'. So what is different? I don't know. It's all a little bit confusing to me...

******

Sometimes I am a bit naughty, well....quite a lot naughty, I suppose. Sometimes I feel cross and I don't know why and I shout and scream and cry a lot and Nanna and Granpa chase me round the room and smack me and tell me I am bad. Sometimes Nanna tells me that if I'm not good I will be put away in a big room that has no doors, no windows, and no way out at all. I see that room in my head all the time. It is a white room with a very high ceiling, but not a very big room, and I sit in the middle, looking up and trying to find even the smallest crack in those shiny white walls. There is no way out, and my inquisitive mind can't help but wonder how I got in there in the first place. How could I get in if there were no doors and no windows? In spite of that, I know that this place exists and that if I am naughty too much more I will go there and nobody will ever hear me cry.

Years later I ask Nanna about this place and ask why she told me that awful story, obviously a lie. She says she doesn't ever recall saying anything remotely like that to me, yet it is still so clear in my head. Even now, all these many years later, I can see that little girl in the middle of that cold, sterile room, and I can feel the absolute fear of abandonment and the hopelessness of never being found and never being heard. Maybe Nanna simply doesn't remember or maybe it is a place that has been imprinted on my mind in other ways. Who knows? All I know for sure is that this sealed white room was part of my waking nightmares for a long time when I was little and I was terrified I would really go there...

Five Years Old...

I am only five years old but I seem to be so much bigger than the other kids, even the older ones in the school. I am tall and I am fat as well. Nobody else seems to look like me at all. I feel so very different from everyone else.

Today I am standing on my own in the middle of the playground, whilst the other kids run around about me, shouting to each other and playing games like 'Tig' and 'What Time Is It, Mr Wolf?' I want to play too, but I'm too scared to ask. I am really shy and it is hard to ask if I can play. Nobody pays much attention to me anyway...

...that is, until the horrible boy in the long, brown duffle coat comes over to where I am standing and starts pointing right at me and laughing.

"Look at her!" he shouts to his friend, and his friend laughs as well. They are both seven, I think. I have seen them sitting in the seven-year-olds' place in assembly. They're only about as tall as I am, but I'm still really scared because they look pretty mean and I don't know what they will do to me.

"Fatso! Fatso!" the duffle coat boy shouts loudly straight at me. His friend comes right up beside me and nips my arm between his fingers, which really hurts and I try to pull away but he has hold of me quite tightly.

"Yuk! Feel all this fat," he says, and they are both pinching me now, over and over. My anorak isn't very thick and I can feel every single pinch. At the same time, they shout right into my face;

"Fatso! Piggy! Fatso! Piggy..."

Other children hear them and come over to join in as well, and I can't shut out the sound of their voices, even when I put my hands tightly over my ears. They just shout even louder anyway and then they try to pull my hands away so I can hear them again.

I don't cry though. I WON'T cry, even though I really really feel like it. I don't want them to make fun of me for THAT, too. And so I just stand there with my eyes squeezed tight shut so I can't see their horrible, mean faces, and I keep my hands pressed on my ears as much as I can, and I hum to myself too—not a song though, just one long low hum so that I can drown out some of their nasty words.

Then the bell rings for the end of playtime and they all run off inside as if nothing has happened. I still keep my eyes tightly shut until it all goes completely silent around me and then I go inside too and get told off by the teacher for being late. My arms hurt from all the nipping and my eyes are sore from squeezing away the tears. And now the teacher doesn't like me either, and calls me lazy and says I should have run faster to get into the classroom on time. The other kids laugh and say I can't run because I am too fat, but the teacher tells them to be quiet and to get on with their work. I wish so much that I could just run out of the door and go home. I hate it here so much.

...The next playtime is just the same, and the next, and the next. Different kids join in each time as they discover the new game. That's all it is to them—a fun game. I know I should ask a grown up for help, but I daren't say anything to anyone at all, and the teacher on duty in the playground never seems to notice or else thinks I am all part of the game as well. Can't she see that I'm not having fun here at all?

I don't even tell Nanna or Granpa at home. I go back to them every day at three o'clock and when Nanna asks if I have had a good day, I just say Yes and she doesn't ask any more, so I don't tell her any more. She would just be cross anyway. She always makes me a cup of tea in my teddy bear mug when I come home and gives me some biscuits to dip into my tea, which I really love doing. She gives me two biscuits to start with, but I always ask for another and another because I like them so much. They seem to make everything better, even if it's only for a little while…

Six Years Old…

I really think that breakfast is my most favourite part of the day. I feel all little and cosy and safe somehow when I am eating my breakfast. I eat just the same food in the exact same way every day and I never ever want it to change.

I have a little yellow wooden stool to sit on that Granpa made by himself, and in front of me I have a bigger yellow wooden stool which is kind of like my table. On top of the bigger stool is a little tin tray, which now has a very faded picture of Mary on it—you know, the one in the nursery rhyme who had a little lamb. But it is a very old tray—I think it used to be my Mummy's—and it has been washed so much that Mary and her lamb have very nearly disappeared. If I squint hard enough with my eyes mostly shut I can just about see where she is though. That's what I do whilst Nanna makes my cup of tea in a morning. I trace round the outside of the lamb and then try to find Mary's face. Then Nanna brings me my breakfast, which is always four biscuits from her big tin on the cabinet. It's always the same, and I love it.

Some of my favourite biscuits are called Safety First and they have all different road signs on them, which I always look at before I eat them. I don't like it if I have two the same and I ask Nanna to swap them for different ones. My other favourites are called Sports biscuits and they have pictures on as well, of people doing all kinds of sports, and they have to be different too.

Sometimes Nanna will give me extra biscuits if I natter at her enough, but not all the time. It depends what mood she is in. I always dip them in my tea—I never just eat them as they are. I love the way they go all soft and kind of melt inside my mouth and I don't like them so much when they are hard and crunchy. Sometimes I leave them in the tea too long by mistake and Nanna has to give me a spoon to fish the soggy biscuit out with. I even eat *that*, as I never want to waste any part of my breakfast.

This is my lovely, warm time of the day before I have to go out to school. I like it even better on the dark winter mornings. I feel as if I am in my own little safe world, sitting on my little yellow stool with my Mary tray, my tea and my biscuits. I am warm, I am safe, and I wish I could stay there forever and never have to go outside at all…

Seven Years Old…

I am so scared and so embarrassed and so ashamed of myself that I want to run away and hide somewhere where no one will ever find me. I am seven and a half years old and I have noticed that two small bumps are beginning to grow on my chest. I don't know what they are as no one else in my class has them. No other children have them anyway, only the teacher and I am sure I am far too young to have THEM. I think I may be ill or something and I am so afraid that something bad is happening to me. What if I'm going to die?

Nanna sees me trying to cover myself up the next time I am having my bath and she says I am starting to 'develop', but I don't know what she means at all. Developing what? What does develop mean anyway?

"You're starting to get a bust," she explains to me and then SHE looks really embarrassed too, and she looks away from me and gets busy finding my towel so that I can get out of the bath.

"But why am I getting a bust NOW?" I ask her, even more frightened than I was before. I thought it might be something the doctors could make go away and then I would be okay again, not a BUST—not something that older people have.

"I'm only seven, Nanna! Nobody else has bumps like me in my class, or even in my whole year. They'll all laugh at me even more now and call me a freak. A bust is for older girls, isn't it, not little girls like me."

But then I'm not really little, am I, and that is the problem…

Nanna says she'll get me a nice bra next time she is at the shops but I'd rather die than wear a bra to school, so I tell her that, and she just tells me not to be silly and that it's quite natural to develop and it had to happen someday. ALL girls end up wearing bras, and as soon as you start developing you have to wear one and that's all there is to it. But I just can't understand it. Why is this happening to me now? If it wasn't such a freaky thing to happen, then other girls my age would have bumps as well, and they just don't.

I want them to go away so badly. I try to push them back in again. I lie hard on my tummy against the floor and try to flatten them down. I even wrap some of Nanna's bandages around my chest really tight and keep them on for ages. I would sleep in them if Nanna wouldn't notice me putting them on, but it wouldn't make much difference anyway because as soon as I take the bandages off the bumps are there again and they never disappear. I just don't know what else to do except cry and cry and cry…and wish and hope that they will go by themselves.

******

…It is PE today and I am so very scared that someone will notice my bumps. Nanna hasn't got me a bra yet, thank goodness, so no one will see that, but we have to do PE in our vest and pants and my bumps show up quite a lot under my vest.

One girl, horrible Amanda, is my partner when we have to do throwing and catching and she looks right at me and asks me what I have got stuffed down my vest. I have no idea what to say her at all and so I blurt out the very first thing that comes into my head.

"It's my lunch." I tell her and she seems to believe me for some reason, even though I know I wouldn't believe it myself. She doesn't say anything else about it then, but she keeps on staring at my chest, and when we have finished PE and go to get changed, I see her whispering to Jenny and Sally, and soon they are looking across at me and giggling behind their hands. I get changed as quickly as I can and rush back to class but I know I have gone all red and I feel like bursting into tears. At that moment if I had a pair of scissors I would cut off my bumps just so that I could be like the other girls and not feel like such an alien, but of course I can't do that and they will never go away again. Nanna told me that for sure. They are here to stay, whatever I do.

From that day on I hate PE, I hate school, I hate those horrible girls, but most of all I hate my cruel, cruel body for all the tricks it is playing on me. I hate myself for being so different. I never ever want to 'develop'—I want to stay a little girl forever and ever and never ever grow up…

******

I hate the darkness. I hate my bedroom. I hate the night. I am so terrified of the blackness around me when Nanna puts out the light at night and I lie there rigid in my bed, just willing myself to fall asleep or wishing the night would fly by and it would be morning again. But the nights never go fast, no matter how hard I wish them to.

Nanna says there is nothing to be afraid of in the darkness, and she makes me look around my room before she switches the light off to prove there is nothing there. I know there is never anything there in the daylight, it is just when all the lights are out that things come. But she doesn't believe me because she can't see anything, and only I can. It's not ghosts or anything, or at least I don't think it is. And it's nothing to do with what I watch on TV or read in books, although I am very afraid of the Daleks on Dr Who. No, I don't know where all these scary things come from and so it is hard to explain to anyone, especially to Nanna.

You see, I have these 'little pictures' which float around my room in the darkness all by themselves. Nanna says I am just imagining them and it is because I read too many stories and think too much about things. People even laugh about it sometimes and my 'little pictures' have become a kind of family joke, as if they don't really matter, but they are so very scary to me. Even when I close my eyes really tight shut, these pictures are still there. Sometimes it can be a person or an animal or just an object, but I can see them clearly with my eyes and in my head and they only go away when *they* want to. I don't seem to have any control over them at all.

One night I see a man sitting by my bed, just sitting there, not even looking at me, and I try with all my might to make him disappear but he just won't go away until he is ready. I can't move at all, I can never go through to Nanna and Granpa's bedroom because I think they will be cross, and besides, I am far too frightened to even climb out of bed. So each night I go through this torment until I eventually fall asleep and when I wake up and it is finally daylight I am so incredibly relieved that I have got through the night safely once more.

Then one day I realise that my 'little pictures' have just gone, all on their own. I even stare into the darkness and see if I can find them again just to make sure, but they are most definitely gone. The fear of the darkness is still there and will be for many years to come, but at least the pictures have gone. I don't know where or how, but they never come back again.

About twenty-five years later, I am staying at my mother's house with my daughter who is about the same age as I was then, and lying there in our beds in the darkness we are talking about the day. Then she tells me about a picture that she can see floating in the black room. Describe it to me, I ask her calmly, but my heart is thumping in my chest as I wonder what is to come. She tells me about a beautiful horse pulling a golden carriage and she describes it in such immense detail and with absolutely no fear in her voice at all. Instead, there is more of a sense of wonderment in her that she can see such beautiful things in the darkness.

I am truly amazed. I have never ever told her about my own 'little pictures' and now she sees them too. What else do you see, I want to know? Tell me about them? So she tells me about the people, the animals and the objects she can see in her room every night, just floating around in the darkness, and I listen in awe. She has no fear at all, they are just something that happens in her life and she accepts them as normal. I tell her I had them too, and it is yet another seal on the close bond we share. But what thrills me even more is the fact that they do not frighten her at all and that she can tell me about them without fear of being ridiculed or disbelieved, and that darkness to her means nothing more than night-time…

Eight Years Old…

Granpa is still at work tonight, at the metal smelting factory—at least I think that's what it's called, but I don't really know what it means. I know he is a boss and he took me to his office once which looked really big and grand but I don't really know what he does. Some days he doesn't come home until after I am in bed and other days he works from very early in the morning and is here when I come home from school. But today he goes to work in the afternoon and it is just Nanna and I tonight for our tea.

Nanna has this huge box of chocolates up on her shelf that Granpa gave her for her birthday back in June and every night she gets it down for us to have two each after our tea. It is one of those really big flat boxes of chocolates with a lovely picture on the front of it and only one massive layer of chocolates inside, and when Nanna gets it down from the shelf and puts it onto the table so we can choose what we'd like, it seems to fill the whole table top. My eyes grow wide as I look across the sea of chocolates and Nanna usually ends up getting cross because I take far too long to choose the two that I really want. It is so very important to me that I find the exact right two that I'd like or else the rest of the night will feel kind of wrong. I don't know why—that is just the way it is. But Nanna doesn't know this and sometimes when she is cross because I take too long, she just hands me the first two she comes to and puts the box away quickly. I can only sit there looking up at the shelf, wishing I could just climb right up and swap the chocolates for the right ones, but I know that Nanna would go mad if she ever found me doing that, so I just have to make do with what I have. Those nights aren't so good though.

Tonight when she puts the chocolate box down on the table and I see the fluffy white cat on the lid, I stop what I'm doing straight away and come across to see what is left.

"Not many to choose from now," Nanna says, opening it up and showing me the contents. "Only six there now, so that's two each for you, Granpa and me."

"But Granpa isn't here, "I point out. "We could have three each, you and I."

"Don't be so greedy," Nanna tells me. "Granpa can have his two when he comes home. Now choose the ones you want and don't take too long about it."

I still take ages to choose, even though there are so few of them to pick from, but at last I take the strawberry cream and the caramel cup. Nanna picks the Turkish delight and the hazelnut truffle. We've left the chewy nougat one and the orange cream for Granpa.

I eat my two chocolates so very slowly—nibbling round the edges to make them last as long as I can, like I always do. I take the tiniest bites possible, but even so, they are both soon gone. They never last long enough. My eyes wander back to the table where the box still sits with its lid on, waiting for Granpa to come home later. Nanna said it wasn't worth putting it back on the shelf with only two sweets in it, and that I can have the picture of the fluffy white cat on the lid once the box is empty. But I don't want the picture...I want those two chocolates that are left, and I want them so badly that when I go back to reading my book, I can't seem to read the words at all, and I can't stop thinking about the chocolates, still sitting there in their box. I have a drink of orange juice, and then a drink of water. I watch TV, I go to my room and play with my toys, but still I can't get the chocolates out of my head. I know they are Granpa's, but I do so wish they were mine.

I feel as if my whole head is going to explode soon as the thoughts build up and up inside. So I go up to Nanna in the kitchen and take a deep breath, then say,

"Do you think I could just have one more chocolate, please? Just one?"

"You know full well there are only two left and they're for Granpa," is her reply and she turns back to the washing up at the sink. But I can't just leave it at that. Something inside me is gnawing away and it feels as if something terrible will happen if I don't have those chocolates right now.

"Please, "I ask again. "Granpa won't mind. He probably doesn't even know they are there. Please can I?"

I don't just *want* the chocolates now, it's as if I really NEED them. I HAVE to have them or...or what? I don't know, but I have this awful feeling that it will be bad. So I natter on and on at Nanna, and in the end she really loses her patience with me and tells me to 'have the blasted chocolates then if I have to."

I hate it when she is cross with me, but right now I don't care. She has said Yes. I take the sweets out of the box quickly before she changes her mind and then go back to my chair in the corner of the room and hide behind my book. I nibble my way around the edges of the chocolates as I did with my own two, but these sweets don't taste as good as I thought they would. Because now I feel so guilty about taking Granpa's chocolates that I simply can't enjoy them the same, even though I know I *had* to have them. Now he won't have any for himself when he comes home and it's all because of me. Nanna is cross with me because I am so greedy, and Granpa doesn't have his sweets any more. I am an absolutely greedy pig, and I am a really horrible person. I know I am...

I finish the chocolates because I have to now that I have them. I couldn't leave them even if they were poisonous, because I made such a fuss about having them, but I feel so very bad inside and I wish I never even seen the rotten chocolate box tonight.

I am eight years old and I have just discovered the power that food can have in my life. It can make you feel oh, so happy but it can also make your heart feel full of tears...

******

One of my very first best friends is called Carrie. We are in the same class at school together and she has this lovely, big family which I would love to be a part of. She has two big sisters and a Mum and Dad and lots of dogs and there is always something going on in her house. I just love spending time there.

Carrie and I spend our dinner times together as well and it is with her that I discover what is to be a secret and shameful pastime of mine for many years to come...shoplifting, stealing, thieving, whatever you want to call it. It is shameful whatever the name and it is my most well kept secret over many years and the part of me that I hate the very most.

One lunchtime Carrie and I are in the newsagent's shop just a minute's walk away from my house, the one that delivers Nanna's papers every day, the one where I am known by my name as I am in there just about every day. The newsagent is a foreign man and he speaks in a way that I can't always understand. He is very tall and a little scary but he has always been nice to me and sometimes he gives me sweets for nothing.

This particular day, for no real reason apart from a dare, we wait until his back is turned and then we steal two packets of the football stickers from his shelves and we leave the shop as fast as we possibly can. We haven't got very far away from the shop though, and we are just starting to open the packets of stickers when we hear a loud voice behind us. It is the newsagent, Mr Jasper, hurrying after us, waving his arms in the air and shouting for all to hear. I panic and throw the stickers into the nearest garden but it is much too late and he has seen them and picks them up again. He shouts and shouts and it all becomes a blur to me, as I am so terrified of what will happen now. He is going to tell Nanna, he says, I should be ashamed of myself, Carrie too, although he doesn't shout at her as much as he doesn't know her. I am nothing better than a common thief. I am bad, I am no good, I am a disgrace to my family. He says more and more things like that until he has had enough and lets us go. We wander slowly back to school and I spend my afternoon terrified of what is to come when I go home. I don't even know why I took the stickers…football means nothing to me. It was just something to take, that's all. For no reason, just something I wanted to do at that moment.

Nanna is waiting for me when I get home and she looks so angry I want to run away there and then. So he has told her…I kind of hoped he would change his mind, but no. Why did I do it? She shouts at me…What did I want them for anyway? Didn't I get enough pocket money to buy whatever I needed? How could I do this to her and Granpa after all they have done for me? I beg and beg her not to tell Granpa as I couldn't bear him to know and she grudgingly agrees because she says it would break his heart if he knew, and that makes me feel even worse, if that is at all possible. I want to crawl away into a hole and die. I feel like the worst person on earth and I know I have done something so terribly wrong…

But…

At the very back of my mind another seed has been planted. When I took those stickers, I experienced a few moments of what I can only describe now as 'fullness'. I had something in my possession that I hadn't had to give anything of myself to get. I had gained something without losing anything, and it didn't matter what I had gained—the actual object was immaterial…the feeling inside was far more important. I didn't realise it at the time but I had become hooked on stealing. I craved that feeling again and again, to feel full, even if only for a few minutes. It would override any knowledge that it was wrong, any fear of being caught, any guilt, any shame, anything at all. Nothing could compete with this desperate need inside me to fill that gaping hole in which ever way I could, and sadly, I had discovered at the age of eight, another very shameful and dangerous way of doing just that…

Nine Years Old…

I am sitting on the toilet in the bathroom upstairs, shivering and shaking like a leaf. I am so afraid of what is happening that I simply can't move at all or make a sound, and I just don't know what I am going to do. You see, there is this awful blood coming out of me…coming out of my…I can't even say it, but I know it must mean that there is something badly wrong with me and I have never been so afraid in the whole of my life. Have I cut myself without knowing? Is something wrong inside me? What have I done? What is happening to me? I am absolutely terrified.

I sit there for what seems like ages, shaking and crying, far too frightened to call out to Nanna because I don't want her to see what is happening to me in case it is all my fault and she is cross with me. I'm so afraid I will get into trouble as I have made quite a mess on my clothes and I remember Nanna once saying that blood doesn't wash out very well. I am even more afraid that something terrible is happening to me and a part of me feels that if I don't know what it is, then it is somehow better. What if I am going to die? I could sit right here and just bleed to death and no one would know until they found me, would they? Is this my punishment for growing up too fast and developing too soon? Has my body stretched too much inside because of all the extra food I have been eating? Has something burst inside me? Am I going to bleed forever? I sit and silently cry and cry and cry some more…

In the end, Nanna shouts up the stairs to me and asks me what on earth I am doing up there as we are meant to be going out to the shops soon. I can't even answer her because I am crying so much and making those horrible sobbing sounds that take your breath away and so she comes up the stairs to see what I am doing. She walks right into the bathroom and finds me still sitting there on the toilet, with a hanky stuffed into my mouth to stop me making any noise.

"What on earth…" she begins then she sees my bloodstained pants and says, "Oh, my God." and looks as if she is going to faint or something.

I am convinced now that I am definitely going to die and I cry even more, but loudly now and I go towards Nanna for a hug. But she is busy raking in the back of the bathroom cupboard and she comes out with a plastic bag full of white towel-like things. She hands them to me and says;

"You'll need one of these. But let's get you cleaned up first."

"What is it?" I ask, still so very afraid. "What is wrong with me?"

"It's nothing to worry about," Nanna tells me. "It happens to all young girls sooner or later. You just happen to be one of the sooner ones. It comes along every month and it keeps on going until you are just a bit younger than I am. It's something that helps you have babies. Here…" she hands me one of the towels and I look at it, not knowing what in earth it is for. "Put this in your pants to catch the blood. Keep yourself clean."

The towel thing is like a long piece of cotton wool and it feels very strange and uncomfortable between my legs. I don't like it at all. I still don't really understand what is going on inside my body and I wish I could ask Nanna more questions, but she is getting busy with my dirty clothes, soaking them in the sink, and she has her 'don't interrupt me just now' face on and I daren't say anything else.

I just go over and over in my head what she has told me. Every month? For how many days every month? All the time? Just a few? And my tummy hurts now as well. Is that normal? Will it always be that way? My head is buzzing with unanswered questions and I feel as if I have become a whole new person in the space of a few minutes. I don't feel like a little girl any more. I don't feel like ME anymore.

Nanna says she will find me a book about what is happening to me. They are called 'periods', these times when I will bleed, which is a funny name to call such a horrible thing, and she also says that I can ask Aunty if I want to know anything else right now. Aunty is a better person to talk about such things, she tells me. She is kind of like a big sister to me. She is twelve years older than me and is Nanna's youngest daughter and she knows all about these things. She has a little baby and she lives with us now. I like Aunty a lot.

There are certain things I must do though, Nanna tells me, when I have these 'periods'. I must never let Granpa know that they are happening, and when I have used these pads I must wrap them up tightly in toilet paper and burn them on the coal fire in the living room, but only when Granpa isn't in the room. I have to wait until he isn't there as he must never know what is happening and must never see what I am doing. I don't know why he can't know…it must really be something quite shameful.

It is a big secret that I can't tell anybody else about. Only me, Nanna and

Aunty will know. It feels as if it is something bad, especially when Nanna tells Aunty about me later in the day and I hear Aunty saying 'but she's so young! It shouldn't have started just yet, should it? "

Once again I feel as if my body is doing something that it shouldn't be doing and somehow that it is my fault. I must be doing something wrong to make all these horrible things happen to me?—first the developing and now these awful periods. Aunty tells me they are a natural part of becoming a woman but how can I be turning into a woman when I am only nine? I am a freak, that is what I am. I bet none of the other girls at school even know about periods, never mind have them themselves. Aunty says they are all to do with babies, but I don't need a baby at my age, and I am so scared that one will start to grow inside me. These periods don't belong in my life, they are dirty and horrible, painful and shameful, and I hate my body for doing this to me. I hate myself for being the sort of person this happens to and I wish I was anybody else but me, I really do…I want to curl up in a cave somewhere and never ever come out again. I want to go back to being little…

Ten Years Old…

I am ten years old, lying in the blackness of my room and my imagination is running riot again. I cannot sleep for imaginary scenarios of all the awful things that could possibly happen in my life playing in my head like a non stop-film. I don't know why I am thinking of these bad things tonight. I don't mean to scare myself this way but it is as if my brain is just running away on its own and I haven't got the power to stop it thinking these awful things.

Right now I am going through what it would be like if Granpa died. What would our lives be like? How would we cope? Would we have enough money? How much would I miss him? How much do I love him? How much does he love me? The thoughts go around and around and I can't stop them, even if I try very hard to think of absolutely nothing. What feels worse is that there is a part of me which actually likes having these thoughts—a part of me feels that if something bad happened in my life, than maybe someone would actually pay attention to me and be nice to me. Maybe I would be noticed, maybe someone would feel sorry for me and put their arms round me and say all those lovely things you see people saying on the TV when someone is sad. I crave this attention and love so much that I try to imagine all the possible ways it would come to me, no matter how horrible it may seem. I create these nightmares for myself and then wish they would go away. I seem to be my own worst enemy.

******

Six months later it is a foggy Wednesday evening at the beginning of December. I usually go to a choir practice in a local church after school on a Wednesday but Nanna has sent a message across to the school to tell me to come straight home because of the fog. It is so thick outside now and the night looks so ghostly and scary. I am glad I don't have to go out anymore.

Granpa is ill in bed as he often is at this time of the year. He gets a lot of chest infections in the cold weather and I have grown used to visiting him in bed, and I like to snuggle up to him and feel the 'prickles' that grow on his chin after he hasn't shaved for a few days. Most years he is poorly over Christmas and my birthday and the New Year as well, and sometimes I get mad at him in my head because Nanna says I can never have a birthday party when Granpa is ill in bed, and I SO want a proper birthday party one day.

This particular Wednesday Granpa gets worse and worse and I am not allowed to go and sit with him as he is coughing so much. In the end Nanna calls an ambulance and I have to sit in the front room and keep out of the way. The whole scene that follows that night remains etched in my mind like a scene from a Halloween movie—the foggy atmosphere outside only adding to the spookiness and the fear that surrounds the whole night.

Nanna and Granpa hardly ever have anyone else in their house but family, as they don't seem to have many friends and so it is strange to see the two large ambulance men in their dark uniforms enter the house by the front door. That is odd in itself because hardly anyone ever uses the front door, and so it is stiff when it is opened and makes a funny noise.

When they come back down the stairs a few minutes later, they are carrying Granpa on a stretcher between them and he is all wrapped up in blankets. All I can see is his face and his eyes are closed as if he is asleep. I peek out from the doorway and wish I could go up and speak to him but I know I wouldn't be allowed, so I just watch as they take him out into the cold, grey night. Some of the fog from the garden curls into the house and I shiver in the biting cold. I hear the ambulance drive away and then there is silence.

Nanna stays at home with Ian and I. Ian is my cousin and he is only a baby, Aunty's baby. Aunty works night shifts at a hospital and Nanna looks after Ian on those nights. That means she can't go to the hospital which is what she really wants to do, I can tell. I am sent off to bed and know no more until the morning, but from what I learn later on, Nanna decides that she has to go to be with Granpa after all. She calls a neighbour to look after Ian and I, she phones for a taxi, but before the taxi has even arrived the hospital has called to say that Granpa has died. It is too late…It is 9.25pm on the night of December 1 and I have lost the only father figure I have ever known.

When I wake up in the darkness of the next morning Aunty is there to tell me that Granpa has died, and I am to take the day off school. From that moment on I have a complete blank in my mind for the rest of that day. I don't know who came to the house, I can't remember if anyone cried or not, I'm sure we did, but I just can't remember anything. I can't even remember my own reaction. All I can recall is the immense guilt that is raging inside me—this is all MY fault. I have imagined this whole story and now it has all come true and Granpa had died because of me. Of course I can't tell anyone this terrible secret or everyone will hate me, even more than I hate myself right now. I say nothing to no one and so nobody is able to tell me that it just isn't true, no way was it my fault and Granpa was a very sick man who would have died no matter what I had imagined all those months ago. To me and for a long long time to come it is MY fault and I drive myself crazy with the guilt.

******

This guilt and the deep sense of loss that I feel at Granpa's death sends my behaviour way over the top for a year or more. I am so angry, so frustrated, so ashamed, so afraid of my own thoughts, but I cannot put these feelings into words at the age of ten and neither dare I tell anyone why I feel this way. I blame myself for every last thing that goes wrong that year and I rage at others because I can't say what I really feel inside. Most of all I shout at Nanna and make her life even tougher than it already is, which just makes me feel even worse. Nanna is so staunch and strong in her grief and in the entire time I live with her I do not see her cry, no matter what is happening. It means that I don't want to cry in front of her either as I feel I must be as strong as she is, and so my grief turns into anger every single day.

People in the family tell me that I have to try my hardest to be good. I have to look after Nanna and be really well behaved for her at this awful time. I am just causing her more pain. I know that, but I just can't stop the way that I am acting and I really wish that I had died too or even instead of Granpa. I simply don't want to BE any more…I have had enough…I don't deserve to live.

Eleven Years Old...

Today I have come away on holiday with my mum and my two sisters. I was so looking forward to this holiday as we are staying in a big caravan which I have never done before, and besides, I have never been on a real holiday where you have to stay overnight and I am really excited about it. Nanna and Granpa and I used to just have days out, not like real holidays though and this one is going to be REAL, like the other kids at school have. We are going to be away for a week and I even get to have my own little bedroom in the caravan!

Mum's friend, Alan, is taking us to the caravan in his car. Gayle and Diane say that he is her boyfriend, but I don't know if that's true. I can't imagine her having a boyfriend and he is really creepy anyway. If she was going to have a boyfriend, she could at least have someone nice. I really really don't like him at all. He is so bossy to us. He tells us what to do all the time, but not like other grown ups do. He tells us what we like and what we don't like. He makes up stupid rules when it isn't even his own house, like he came to my house once and wouldn't let us watch TV when we were eating. Nanna and Mum just let him get away with it too! He decides what programmes we CAN watch, what we should eat, what we should say and do, and I hate it that he is that way to me as well, as I don't even live with Mum. He can pretend to be Gayle and Diane's Dad if he wants but I don't want him to be mine. But I can't say anything, as everyone seems to like him, so as usual, I stay quiet.

When we get to the caravan, Mum says she has a surprise for us. We are all really excited and wonder what it can be. The holiday is good enough, but a surprise as well?

"Alan is staying with us for the week", she tells us and we try not to look disappointed. How can that be a surprise? Even Gayle and Diane don't really like him, but they pretend harder than me to like him because they live with Mum and so they have to.

"It'll be great," Mum tells us. "Alan can take us out in the car every day."...Great...

It is KIND of fun, but not as fun as I thought a holiday should be. Alan makes us all write a diary every day of what we have done and he reads it every night to make sure we have done it right. It is like being at school, except worse because I don't really know what he wants us to write.

Worse than that though are the strange games that he plays with us. He makes up all the rules, of course, and they are always made so that HE can win and we lose, and then he has to punish us. He chases us around the fields outside the caravan and puts nettles down our backs and then tells us not to be silly when we cry. He hits us with coat hangers if we lose. His games aren't fun and we hate playing them but Mum seems to think it is good that he spends time with us. I want to go home, and I wish for the holiday to be over. Mum seems to like Alan, but we all hate him and wish that he had never come with us...

******

I have walked across to my Mum's house today to see Gayle and Diane and to stay for tea as well, but as soon as I walk in, I know that Alan is there as well. He smokes and the kitchen is full of the smell of his rotten cigarettes. Granpa used to smoke as well, but he used to make his own cigarettes with some tobacco out of a tin and they smelt different to Alan's. His are horrible, just like him.

He is playing his stupid games again whilst Mum does the washing up and of course I am told to join in. Mum seems to think it is fun for us. I don't know how she can't see what he is really like. Today's game is just the same as all the others and I lose. He has to think of my punishment, he says, and I cringe as I wonder what he is going to do today. It would almost be easier if he just hit us and then you would know what to expect but he always has to think of something really strange and different. At last he decides that I am to sit on the floor with my legs stretched out in front of me and he will stand on my lower legs, all his weight, just stand there on my legs for a whole minute. Gayle and Diane just look at me and Mum doesn't even seem to notice what is happening.

"Put your legs out," he orders me and I do it, because I don't know what else to do. He carefully stands on my calves, one heavy boot on each leg and balances there, looking at his watch so that he can make sure he does it for a whole minute exactly. He isn't a very tall man but he is quite chunky and he is very heavy to me. I have to stay quiet, I mustn't complain, however much it hurts. Nobody else does or says anything and the minute seems to last forever. Nobody dares talk. Alan is the boss in this house. When he finally steps off me with a smile, I stagger to my feet and run out into the garden, hardly able to feel my legs now. I curl up in a ball at the end of the garden and burst into tears, hugging my poor sore legs to my chest and feeling my heart fill with such hatred that I don't know what to do with it. Nobody comes out to see how I am, and through the kitchen window I can see Mum still doing the washing up. It is as if nothing has happened…and when I eventually go back in, it is only to find that Alan has thought of another game…

"Come and join in," he says…

******

It is six months after this and Alan has stopped coming to see us anymore. I am really happy about that but don't really understand what has happened. A part of me hopes that he is dead, but then I feel so guilty for even thinking that way and when Nanna sits me down one day to talk about Alan, I am terrified that he has been killed and it is all my fault again, like with Granpa.

But it's not that at all. Nanna is so embarrassed by what she has to tell me that she can barely bring herself to say the words at all. Gayle and Diane have been staying at Alan's house some weekends and he has been making them sleep in his double bed with him and he has been touching them in places that he shouldn't. Nanna doesn't tell me anymore and I daren't ask anything more as she looks so uncomfortable, so I just have to use my imagination for the rest. I don't know much about stuff like that, but at school they have told us about staying away from strangers and always telling if someone tried to touch us…you know, THERE. Is that what Nanna means? Has Alan been doing THAT?

Next time I go to Mums house she carries on as if nothing has happened but as soon as I can get Gayle on her own I ask her about Alan and she says it is true. He made them take off their pyjamas and let him touch them and then they had to touch him too. He told them not to tell, and they wouldn't have but Diane said something by mistake and then it all came out. Mum has told him that he can't come round to see them anymore. I think she should have told the police but Gayle says that she didn't want to get Alan into big trouble. If it had been me, I would have made sure he was locked up for ever.

Now I hope more than ever that Alan dies, and I don't care how mean it sounds. Why should good people like Granpa have to die and people like Alan get to stay alive? Granpa never hurt anyone—it's so unfair. And why did Alan do it anyway? He is a grown –up! Mum should never have let him get away with the games he used to play with us, then maybe he wouldn't have gone on to play THOSE kind of games as well. I am just so glad that I live with Nanna otherwise maybe I would have had to go and stay with him as well.

******

And now it is only a few weeks later and when I go over to Mum's house, he is there again, sitting at the kitchen table with a cigarette in his hand and a horrible smirk on his face. I am struck dumb, as he is the last person I ever expected to see there again. I know Mum didn't have him arrested like I would have done and thrown into jail, but I never thought she would want to see him again, but here he is. I stare at him, as if I am just imagining it.

"What's the matter with you?" he asks me. "Cat got your tongue?"

I don't answer; I can't speak. I look over at Mum but she looks away from me quickly. How can she let him back here after what he has done? I don't understand any of it. I thought Mums and Dads were supposed to protect their children. It all seems wrong to me, but there seems to be nothing I can do but just carry on as if it is normal, just like everyone else is doing.

I walk through into the living room where Gayle and Diane are watching TV.

"What's HE doing here again?" I whisper to them as I sit down beside them.

"Mum missed him, I think," Diane told me. "She called him up yesterday." There is a pause, then, "Look what he bought us!!"

There are two brand-new Barbie's up sitting on the settee, complete with half a dozen outfits each. "Aren't they great? Want to play?"

I shake my head and pretend I am interested in the programme on TV. It is ages until I have to go home and I count the minutes as they drag slowly by, all the time praying that today there will be no more of Alan's 'games'…

Twelve Years Old…

I am twelve years old and I still don't know where I came from, why I live with my Nanna, why Gayle and Diane live with my Mum but I never did, or what happened to my Dad, if I ever had one. I ask Nanna occasionally but she always just tells me that I will find out when I am 'older'. I am left with this constant nagging fear that something terrible happened when I was a baby and she can't possibly bring herself to tell me about it. What can be so bad about my past that it has to remain hidden from me until that magical day when I am 'older'? My imagination works overtime as usual and I spend many hours at night trying to work things out, but I never can, and I am too frightened to keep on asking. I start to fear being 'older' because even though I am desperate to know what happened to me, I am also terrified of finding out the truth. At least right now I can still pretend it was something good, but when I know the truth I won't have that chance any more.

Then one day it happens…I am at last old enough in Nanna's eyes to know the truth. She just sits me down and hands me a well-worn plastic bag and inside this bag are the answers to some of my hundreds of questions, all there in black and white. In newspaper cuttings, photographs, police documents, statements, countless articles….all covered with the names of my parents, with photos of me, my name, my OLD name at least, the one I was christened with as opposed to the one I now use every day.

I simply don't know what to make of these answers, it is all too much, and I turn to Nanna for help, but she feels she has done all she can by giving me the information and I can see that she just doesn't want to talk about it. A volcano has just erupted in front of my eyes, but I am to pretend that I didn't see it or feel its impact and carry on as normal.

Except nothing can be normal ever again. I stare at these stark, inhuman cuttings and try to take in the enormous fact that this is MY life, MY beginnings, MY family, MY parents. Names just jump out at me. MY name, HER name, HIS name. I have known nothing about my father all my life and yet suddenly he has a name and a story. He is the man that so detested my crying and the responsibility of having a wife and a child to support that he persuaded my mother to leave me, abandon me as a seven-month old baby, and not only do it once, but twice. They had dreams of a new life for themselves in London, they figured someone else would look after me and that I would be better off without them.

First they left me in my pram outside an amusement arcade, left with nothing but a note pinned onto me like Paddington Bear. 'Please look after this baby'. The police soon found my parents though and I was reunited with them, amazingly enough. Only for them to try again and this time they were a lot more successful in their escape. My mum left me in the waiting room at the local railway station, asked a lady if she would look after me whilst she went to the bathroom and then disappeared onto the next train for London. It took the police a few days to catch up with them this time, but they did and they were both jailed for abandoning me, and I was placed in a childrens' home until it could be decided where I should go next. After a little while, my grandparents were allowed to bring me home with them, and after four lengthy years they finally adopted me. In the meantime I find out that my parents came out of jail, got back together again and had two more children before my father had finally had enough of family life for good and he went back to Canada where he had come from in the first place.

Nanna doesn't know where he is now and says she doesn't ever want to know as it was all his fault. He was a bad man, my mother should never have married him, they told her that, and she doesn't want to hear his name even mentioned in the house. I am not to go bothering my Mum with questions either as it all happened a long time ago now and I shouldn't go raking up the past. She just thought I should know, that is all, and now that I know, I should try to put it behind me like everyone else has. But it is not that easy at all…far from it.

These bare black and white facts paint my life, and I simply cannot grasp what it all means to me. I have so many questions, I need to ask why, I need to know so much more but it seems that all the doors are closed now. I know what happened, that should be enough, Nanna seems to think, but it can never be enough for me, and these questions haunt me. I turn in on myself, thinking it was somehow MY fault, why didn't they want ME? Why did they keep Gayle and Diane but get rid of ME? If only I could ask these questions out loud, them maybe they wouldn't drive me crazy, and maybe I could start to feel a little better about myself instead of spiralling down into self-destruction as I begin to do. All I know for sure is how I feel deep inside…I have such a sense of worthlessness, of being rejected, a feeling that I don't really matter in this world and that no one will ever be there for me, no matter how hard I cry…

Thirteen Years Old…

I am in the middle of watching 'Coronation Street' when the telephone rings. Nanna shows no sign of moving and so I get up and answer it, half expecting it to be my Mum who calls Nanna every night without fail. Instead it is a strange female voice that I have never heard before…she is foreign, American I think at first, and she drawls my name out over the phone.

"I'd like to speak to 'Ayannne'?" she says and I wonder who on earth this is. Some kind of market researcher perhaps? But they never usually ask for me.

"This is Anne speaking," I tell her and the next thing she says nearly has me on my knees in shock.

"Oh, good. Would you like to speak to your father? I have him right here with me."

I cannot speak for what seems like several minutes, but it is probably only a few seconds. Would I like to speak to my father? My *father*? This mysterious figure who has never been a part of my life, and who left so many unanswered questions behind him…do I want to speak to him? NOW?

I stand there petrified, my back to Nanna, trying not to let her see the panic that is rushing through my whole body at that moment. She mustn't know what is happening. No way would she let me speak to him. She hates him, and she wants ME to hate him too.

"Yes," I answer, in the tiniest voice and the next thing I hear is a man's voice on the line—it just has to be HIM.

"Hello, Anne. This is your Dad."

For so long I have dreamed of this moment, meeting him at last, talking to him, having a REAL Dad in my life, and yet now it is happening I am speechless, I am stage struck and I want to hang up, my feelings are so raw. It feels as if I have fallen into some kind of time warp, or have found myself in a movie of someone else's life. All my life I have dreamed of having a Dad, of being like the other kids, of him showing up one day and wanting to be with me, of him saying sorry that he left me and that it was all one huge mistake, and how he wants more than anything to make it up to me. And now here he is, and I just can't take in the enormity of it all.

I can barely speak properly but I know I have to carry on as normal so that Nanna doesn't get even an inkling that something is amiss. So I struggle with words and find some, although I have no idea if what I say makes any sense at all. We talk for four and a half minutes exactly; I see every second of this precious conversation tick by on my watch and I try to remember every word of it so that I can replay it over and over in my mind later on. He asks if I want to meet him and of course I say, Yes! How could I NOT want to meet him? He is my Dad…My Dad!! Wow…MY DAD. So we arrange a time and place and I hang up, feeling as if my world had just tilted on its axis and something so huge has happened to me that I want to shout from the rooftops. My palms are sweaty and my heart is pounding…

"Who was that?" Nanna asks…

I amaze myself by lying so convincingly.

"Just Julie," I tell her. Julie is my best friend at school just now and also a distant cousin. "We're meeting tomorrow night at seven in the Square. Just for a chat."

Nanna grunts and goes back to the TV, suspecting nothing. I feel a surge of guilt for deceiving her but she would never in a million years agree to me meeting my father and I just HAVE to do it. I have to find out for myself what he is really like and where I really come from…

******

I hardly sleep that night and the next day at school is spent daydreaming, playing through all kinds of possibilities in my mind. What will he be like? I bet he's tall because the three of us girls are tall. Dark haired as well for the same reason. What will his life be like? Maybe he will want me to go to Canada and live with him? Or at least go for a holiday…..wow, would I want to go? It could be a whole new life for me. He is married again now; that was his wife on the phone to me last night, Eve, she is called. She is my stepmother…what an odd thought. I actually have a stepmother. I wonder if they have children together. Maybe I have new brothers and sisters. That would just be perfect, like a REAL family at last. A new mum and dad, a new family in a whole new country….

Then I feel so damn guilty for even thinking that way after all that Nanna has done for me—how could I even think of leaving her…Still, dreaming is sooooo very good…And you never know, do you…

******

Then before I know it, it is seven o'clock that night and I am standing in The Square with my friend, Julie. I have asked her to come along with me anyway, just in case. I mean, I know it won't happen but what if he tries to.... I don't know, kidnap me or something? It would be so silly to meet him without somebody else there as well and I can trust Julie not to tell anyone at all. Not that Julie, who is four feet nine inches tall and about six stone soaking wet is going to be much use to me if he tries to abduct me, but I feel better just having her there.

I do wish other people were on time though. I have got there early so I wouldn't miss him, and it is well after seven now and there is no sign of anybody remotely resembling a man looking for his long lost daughter. It is driving me crazy.

I walk up and down in front of the bus shelter where we have arranged to meet and I just *will* him to turn up before I explode inside. My nerves are wound up so tightly with anticipation that I am sure I will have a heart attack very soon if…

And then suddenly he is here…And I stare and stare intently at this man as I see my father for the very first time. It's the first time that I can remember anyway, and I try to take in everything that this moment means to me. He is tall and dark haired, just as I thought he would be, and his face has a lop-sided appearance to it. Right now he is frowning and looking as if he would rather be anywhere else on earth than here, as he seems so very awkward and ungainly. He doesn't look like me, or at least I don't look like him. Is this really him? We look at each other nervously as he climbs off the bus that has brought him here, and it seems forever before one of us makes a move. I desperately want him to run towards me, pick me up in his arms and swing me round and round. I want him to hug me and kiss me and tell me how much he has missed me and will never let me out of his life again…but real life is so very different. As always.

"Are you Anne?" he asks, almost distantly, coldly, as if he is meeting a business client for lunch. He doesn't even make a move towards me, just stands there as the bus pulls away behind him. All I can do is nod back.

"Okay, then…" is all he can reply. "How about we find somewhere to eat?" Then he sees Julie beside me. "Is this Gayle?"

"No, no…" I stutter, awkwardly. "This is my friend, Julie. Is it okay if she comes with us as well?"

He doesn't look too pleased and my heart sinks as my dream of how this night would be slowly dissolves in front of my eyes.

"Okay, I suppose so," he says, and we get back on the next bus into the town where he is staying in a city centre hotel with Eve. But it is all so very wrong, and I want to be anywhere but here right now. It feels as if someone has handed me a treasure chest and I have opened it, only to find that it is empty after all. My dad can barely look at me as we sit side by side on the bus. He sits as far away from me as he can, so that we don't even touch, and he drums his fingers on his knees throughout the journey and never says a word. I keep waiting for him to talk to ME—HE is the grown up, He is the one who left ME, not the other way round. Surely it should be him who tries to make it all okay? Who starts up the conversation. Who asks how I am. How I have been all these years. TALK TO ME!!!!, I want to scream at him.

We get off the bus in silence, walk to his hotel in silence and eat a meal of greasy burger and chips in silence. Well, maybe there are a few words here and there, but nothing of any consequence and I feel as if I could be sitting with anyone in the whole world, not someone I am actually connected to in any way. Stuff like, How is school, what grade are you in, what subject do you like best? Not, what has your life been like for you since I left you? How has it affected you? Do you know how sorry I am for what I did?

Then we go up to his room and meet his wife. She is a small, dark haired lady who reminds me of a witch. She has an abrupt manner about her, and a kind of twitchiness, which makes me even less at ease than I was before. Once again I am afraid and wonder what is going to happen next. I should never have come up to his room. Eve asks me if I have ever flown before...This is madness, I have to get out of here fast. I should never have come here. He was never going to be what I wanted him to be, otherwise why would he have left in the first place?

There are no kidnap attempts though, nothing happens at all after that. He takes a couple of photos of me, standing there in my black duffle coat with my long hair spread around my shoulders. He says he loves my hair...He loves long hair...He gives me his address in Canada, I give him another friend's address so he can write to me too, as no way could he send anything to my house or Nanna would have a fit. We say goodbye, still never touching and Julie and I catch the bus back home.

Three days later I have my hair cut short...very short.

Fourteen Years Old...

I am sitting here in my bedroom, in floods of tears, wishing that I could just disappear off the face of the earth somehow and never come back to this god-awful life. Nanna is so very angry with me right now and I know she just keeps on blaming me for what is happening, but how can it possibly be my fault? I just wish she would stop shouting at me and shaking her head in despair and just give me a hug, but that will never happen.

We have just had three taxis in a row showing up at our door, all of them from different companies and none of which were actually ordered by Nanna or I. Yesterday we were sent the bill for a huge bouquet of flowers that I had supposedly ordered to be sent to a boy in the fifth year that I have a crush on. I swear I didn't do any of it, and I THINK Nanna believes me, but she is still so angry with me because I have brought all this trouble to her door, so she says. I am sure I know who is behind all this though and right now I could kill her stone dead. It is Emma, a girl at school who is making my life a real misery right now, and I hate her with every fibre of my being.

She only came to our school a year ago, having moved here from up near Newcastle. She knew nobody here at all, so my best friend, Nicky, and I took her around with us and made her feel really welcome. For a short while it was the three of us who were good friends, but very soon I began to feel pushed out and it was increasingly obvious that Nicky and Emma wanted to be by themselves. And soon they were, and I was on my own again.

Since then Emma has made it her life's work to make me unhappy and she is really succeeding as well. She makes fun of my size, my background, of my glasses, of the fact that I am clever and answer questions in class, of anything she can think of really. And worse than that, she gets other people to join in; people I once considered to be friends of mine. One day she told me I was a total nonentity, which meant absolutely nothing to me at the time, except that I knew it couldn't possibly be a compliment coming from her. I looked it up in the dictionary as soon as I got home and found out that it was 'a person or thing of no importance, non-existence, non-existent thing'. That describes just perfectly how I feel about myself right now and it hurts like hell that Emma can reach right into my soul that way and find the very thing that would hurt me the most. Is it really that obvious to her? Who else can see that I am one big Nothing?

I feel as if I have a vast emptiness inside me; there is no real life, no spark, nothing that remotely appeals to anyone else. I have no confidence. No guts to stand up for myself. I just sit there and take all the hateful words and comments that Emma throws at me and I never even retaliate. I can never think of a single thing to say back to her and that makes me hate myself even more. I am a sitting target for her, a toy, a hobby, a bit of fun, but essentially in her eyes, and in mine as well, I am a big fat Nothing. A Nonentity.

The very worst thing for me is that there is no one to talk to about the way I am feeling and I do feel so very alone. Nanna is so upset and angry about the taxis and the flowers, oh…and also the funny phone calls we have been getting which I am sure are down to Emma as well. I feel like Nanna blames me for it all, and I just don't want to make things any worse by trying to discuss it with her. She still hasn't got over Granpa's death properly and she is a lot more remote from me than she used to be.

I can't cope with this anymore, I really can't. I wish to God I never had to set foot outside this bedroom again—I wish that I could just hide myself away from the world and never get hurt again. But Nanna insists that I go to school, of course, and I am so scared of the consequences if I decided not to turn up.

I am one of the Good Girls, always have been. So I am reduced to making up strategies to get myself through the days instead. Coping mechanisms of a sort. I make myself out a chart with every single lesson I have to endure before the start of the Christmas holidays. Eight lessons a day, five days a week, nine weeks to go....that's 360 lessons until I will be free of Emma, at least physically free of her for two whole weeks, although I know that her insults and mocking sneers will still be rooted in my head. I put a capital 'E' next to every lesson on my timetable that Emma shares with me. She doesn't take every subject that I do, thank goodness, and so I get a reprieve from her here and there, but not enough to make the days really bearable.

Tomorrow is only Wednesday...how I wish it were Friday...and I have to go to school and see Emma and Nicky sniggering at me as they discuss the taxi scam they have obviously cooked up between them. If I had the guts, I would end it all tonight, I really would. I would swallow some lousy pills and end it all. I could—they are sitting right there by my bed. But I don't have the nerve. Instead, I sneak downstairs whilst Nanna is in the bathroom and grab a handful of biscuits and a Mars bar. It's the only way I can even begin to quiet my mind right now...

Fifteen Years Old...

Aunty and the two children she now has are living with us again and the atmosphere in the house is absolutely crazy. Ian is four years old and Joanne is only a baby, just a year old. They have been living in a flat in the town for a while now but they had to move out and this is the only place Aunty could go so quickly. I hide away in my room most of the time that I am home, whilst the children shout and scream downstairs, and Aunty tries to keep them quiet. My bedroom is my only refuge, as much as a room without a lock CAN be. I can put on my stereo, plug in the headphones and shut out the outside world as I drown in beautiful music.

I really hate living here right now. The atmosphere is forever tense, as Aunty and Nanna clash on a regular basis. They are either fighting or ignoring each other, and no way is there enough room for us all in this pokey little council house. There are two adults, a teenager and two very active children living here and we are all sharing a small two bed roomed house, with only one living room and a little kitchen and bathroom. There really feels as if there is nowhere to go some days, especially when the kids find their way up to my room and play there. We fall over each other all the time.

Nanna gets so upset and angry when the kids scratch a piece of furniture with their toys, or when they tear a book that she has had for years, which maybe one her own children used to read. She and Granpa bought all the furniture in the house when they first married and she feels as if her life is being eroded piece by piece. She doesn't tell me this, of course, as we never speak about it, but I can see it in the pained expression in her eyes, and it makes me want to put it all right for her but I simply can't. I am always so damned powerless.

The fights between Nanna and Aunty are becoming so petty as well. Nanna says that Aunty is drinking too much of the coffee and she can't keep on affording to replace it, so she has hidden the jar of coffee upstairs in the bedroom and if I want any I have to sneak a cup when Aunty is out or asleep. I am sure she can smell it anyway and I feel like a guilty thief just for having a cup of coffee in my own house.

Aunty says that Nanna watches her every move and is always interfering when it comes to disciplining the children. She says Nanna doesn't have the right to be so judgmental and Nanna says that she does all the time they are living under HER roof.

They fight over what TV programmes we all want to watch, what food we eat, when we cook the meals, who does the washing, who has used up the last of the wash powder, who irons the clothes—just anything you can think of and then some. They are so venomous that you would never think they were mother and daughter and that they once had a love for each other. Maybe they still do, but I can't see it at all. Not now. I try to keep out of the way as much as I can, as I love them both and can't stand to see what they are doing to each other. I am constantly waiting for the next fight to erupt and I can never relax and never feel at peace when I am at home.

I hate to come home from school these days, no matter how much I hate going there as well. I never quite know what I will find when I walk in the door.

Today is the very worst day of all up to now. I walk in to find Nanna furiously washing up at the sink in the kitchen, the plates crashing against each other as she thrusts them onto the draining board. She barely looks up when I say Hello and I know straight away that something bad has happened.

The house is very still and there is no sign of Aunty and the children. They are usually in when I come home from school as they have their tea not long after that, so it is odd that they aren't here. It is pouring with rain outside as well, so I doubt they have gone for a walk. I want that moment to freeze in time right there and then, as I am so afraid to ask Nanna what has happened and to actually find out. These days are so very unpredictable that it could be anything and the fear in my stomach ties me up in knots. As if she can read my mind, Nanna turns round very slowly and says;

"She hit me."

Her voice is so low and she sounds so defeated that I can hardly bear to look at her. I look down at her arm, which she is holding out towards me, and I can see an enormous purple bruise beginning to develop on the top of her upper arm. I want to scream and scream and run and run but I am rooted to the spot and I can't even bring myself to speak. The emotions swirling round inside me like a dust storm stick in my throat and I feel so very sick.

"I hit her too, though. I'm just as bad as she is." She takes a very deep breath and I can see that she is fighting away the tears. "She called me an evil old witch…my own daughter called me an evil witch…"

At last I am able to move and I hug her so tight and cry so hard that I feel as if I will die right there and then. It is too much, far too much for any of us. I feel so incredibly trapped her, drowning in quicksand with no way out. There is nowhere to go, nowhere to hide, no peace, no freedom, no space, no time, no happiness, nowhere to go without fear following right behind me. I have nowhere to go. I have no rights anymore in this house. I have to give in to the whims of the children just to keep the peace, I have to try and make everyone happy, I have to try and be friendly towards everyone, I can't do this any more…

I stop crying at last and Nanna pulls away. She has stayed strong all the time, she hasn't cried, she is as stoical as always, resolved, determined just to carry on, and I must do the same.

"Put the kettle on," she tells me. "We'll have a cuppa before they come back. I got some more biscuits this morning…get them out of the cupboard, will you?"

I wipe my eyes, and prepare to stuff it all back down once more…

Sixteen Years Old…

I am rushing around the house like a mad thing, trying to get myself ready before I go out. As usual I have spent ages up in my bedroom trying on different outfits then hurling them across the floor because they simply don't fit. How can I have put on so much weight so fast? I try to diet, I really do, but it never seems to get very far—and this is what I get for it. Trousers that won't fasten, skirts with waistbands that dig tightly into me, jumpers which fit me like a second skin….How could I possibly have let myself go this way?

Okay, so I don't exercise very much and I do love my food. In fact I would go as far as to say that I desperately NEED my food for more than just feeding my body. It means far more to me than that at this point in time. And I admit here and now that I have started to sneak extra food into the house and I eat it in the relative peace of my bedroom last thing at night when everyone else is asleep. Some nights I even try to hide a bar of chocolate behind a book I am reading and nibble at it when I hope Nanna isn't looking. God, I hope she never sees me. I am so damned ashamed of what I do and she thinks badly enough of me as it is. She is such a small eater and always looks at me disapprovingly when I eat more than she does. Which is every single day without fail.

At last I find a pair of awful brown trousers that used to be Aunty's and which only just fit me if I breathe in enough. I also come across a polo neck jumper which doesn't match the trousers at all and certainly doesn't do my ever increasing figure any favours but I have no choice if I ever want to go out tonight. I slip a black jacket over the top of my outfit in the hope that it'll hide the bits that I don't want anyone to see. Some hope, but I try.

Nanna is reading a book when I go downstairs and she looks up at me just in time to see me lifting up my jumper to pull on a loose thread hanging from the waistband of my trousers. I have exposed the roll of fat that hangs over the top of my trousers and which I spend most of my waking days trying to hide from the world. I pull my jumper down fast but it is too late.

"You're fairly piling on the weight, aren't you?" Nanna says and then goes back to her book as if she has just casually remarked on the weather rather than shaken the whole of my soul to the core. She's NEVER commented on my weight before, maybe my behaviour or what I say, but never on my weight. She's always said I looked just fine, even when it was blatantly obvious to me that I looked huge and disgusting, but tonight…why tonight? Why did she say that to me tonight?

I don't answer her, I can't. I walk slowly back upstairs, take off my clothes and climb into bed, covering myself up completely with the blankets and wishing that I could make myself really disappear just as easily. I sob and sob until I have nothing left inside me. Then I fall into oblivion and sleep.

By the morning I seem to have turned the utter pain and despair that I felt last night into a ball of anger and hatred towards myself and the world at large. I sit up in bed and swear to myself there and then that I WILL lose the weight this time. I'll show them.... I never ever want to hear those words said to me again, and feel this desperate pain and rejection, this self-hate, this disgust at who I am. Never again.

Today I will go on yet another diet but this time it will be different. This time it will work.

This time it will change my life for good...

Chapter Two

I Want to be Little Again

Minus Five Pounds...

The first few days of a diet are always somewhat like a spiritual experience for me. I feel so high, so in control, so cleansed, so positive—as if my whole world has suddenly balanced itself and I am pointing most definitely in the right direction at last. THIS is where I feel most at home in my life. THIS is where I am meant to be.

I have tried many different diets before this one. None of them have been exactly successful or I wouldn't be where I am today! It always feels great for the first few days then I usually succumb to the hunger pangs and abandon the diet by the wayside in favour of some chocolate biscuits or a couple of slices of cake. But THIS time feels so very different. I can't explain why really, as I'm not doing anything out of the ordinary compared to the other times. I mean, I've cut down my calorie intake to a thousand calories a day, although I try to eat less if at all possible. I have made myself out a chart so that I can tick off all the days that I am 'Good' and see them building up before my eyes, giving me a real sense of achievement. I have made up a fifteen-minute exercise routine and I go through it faithfully every evening—a lot like all the other times I have tried to lose weight. But there is a greater sense of impetus behind this current diet somehow. Everything in my life at present seems to hinge on this diet being a success—every aspect of my pitiful life will be made so much brighter and more bearable if this diet really works out for me and I can lose this weight once and for all.

Right now I am under so much pressure at school to pass my 'O' level exams and do really well with them. Everyone just presumes that because I am bright I will automatically pass them with high marks, but I certainly don't have that kind of confidence in my academic abilities. I wish there was just ONE person who believed me when I tell them I am afraid I may fail. Mostly people just laugh and say;

"Yeah, right! You KNOW you'll pass, no bother!"

But you see I DON'T know that at all and this fear of failure that I live with every day is driving me crazy. When everyone just presumes you will succeed in everything you do, then the fear of failure becomes far more intense. It is a huge Unknown. What if I don't pass? What will they think of me THEN?

I still don't have a best friend at school following all the hassle with Emma, which has thankfully died down a little bit now. She has found easier prey in another new girl who is extremely quiet and wears a huge brace. I would love a very best friend to confide in, but most girls tend to shy away from the people who are picked on, just so that they don't have to go through the same things themselves. I wish I could just be normal. I would love to be one of those girls who seem to fit in so easily. Someone who is readily accepted by everyone and who is right there in the centre of every group instead of on the outside as I tend to be. What I wouldn't give for a REAL best friend right now. I just want to be a part of the life that is going on around me and not feel like the big fat freak that I am.

And as for my home life…well, that is no better at all. Aunty is still living with us, as she can't find anywhere she can afford to move to with the children. She and Nanna are either fighting or completely ignoring each other, depending on what stage of a fight they are at. I have hardly any peace to revise for exams as the kids are always there, and they are never quiet unless the TV is on, and that doesn't make for a peaceful atmosphere for me at all. There is no sense of safety at home, no security, no knowledge that I can shut myself away and not be interrupted at all. I feel as if I am forever on alert, waiting for another fight to break out or for one of the kids to scream and start another tantrum, as they invariably do. They are stressed out by living this way as well and I really feel for them too, but I can't be there for everyone. I can never just rest and BE these days and I yearn for some peace in my head. I feel like the noise never stops.

On a more personal level, I completely hate myself at this point in time. I hate my body most of all. I hate how disgustingly fat it is, how saggy it is, how desperately unfit it is when I exert myself, how all the fat concertinas up when I sit down, how I can't find decent fashionable clothes to fit me, how people at school STILL make fun of me and call me names. But most of all I hate the fact that up until now I have done sod all to make it any better for myself. What have I done? A few half-hearted diets here and there, that's all. But I am always so damned weak that I can't even stick to them for more than a few days without giving in to my greed. Even if I tell myself over and over that feeling slimmer and healthier is so much more important than having that particular chocolate bar or whatever may be tempting me right there and then, it STILL doesn't get through to me. It seems to me that I am so pathetic that I would rather eat the chocolate than improve my life, and what on earth does that say about who I really am?

So, THIS time feels like a last ditch attempt to put my life back on track (if it has ever been there in the first place!) and to really make a difference to how I feel. I have to do everything in my power to make this one work, and it feels as if my whole life depends on it somehow. If I don't lose weight this time, then I will always be that Nonentity that Emma says I am. I will never be accepted by anyone in the way that I truly want to be, and I will certainly never be able to like myself in any way, shape or form.

I want this diet to be The One—the one that chases away the demons, and all the fears, the sleepless nights, the shame, the guilt, the cravings, the desperation, the loneliness—the one that makes it okay just to be ME.

It simply HAS to work this time…there is no other way…

Minus Ten Pounds…

Wow—this diet is going far better than any I have ever been on before and I am so pleased when I weigh myself to find that I have lost ten whole pounds up to now! That's more than I have ever lost before and it is a great start to it all.

I am so proud of my willpower these days as well. Take today for instance; Mum, Gayle and Diane have come over for their tea and Nanna suggests that we all have a takeaway—Fish and Chips—to save her having to cook. I haven't been eating meals properly over the past two or three weeks anyway, with being on my diet and I have cut down a lot, so I don't even realise that I have been included in the invitation at first. Instead I go about getting my crispbreads and low fat cheese spread out of the cupboard for my own meal. I find a low fat black cherry yoghurt for my pudding as well. I have worked out all the day's calories already this morning and charted them so that I can't get caught out and eat too much.

"How about a bit of fish for you, Anne?" Nanna asks, as I am hunting for a knife. "You've barely eaten all day and those things certainly won't fill you up."

But I shake my head firmly and say, "I can't. I'm not that hungry anyway.

And besides—the Fish and Chips from that shop are just dripping in fat. They make me feel sick."

It is a blatant lie, but there is no way I could even contemplate eating something like that. I can't even have an extra bite of anything that isn't written up on my chart. I have to be really rigid about this diet to make it work properly and I am committed to it like never before.

Mum takes some money from Nanna and goes across to the Fish and Chip shop behind our house, and Gayle comes into the kitchen and watches me smearing the cheese spread over the crispbreads as thinly as I possibly can. She has an undisguised look of distaste on her face.

"Is that all you're having?" she asks. "They look gross. Like cardboard."

"They're lovely," I insist. "Much better for you than Fish and Chips any day."

But even *I* don't convince myself, especially when Mum walks back in with those delicious smelling packages in her hands. Fish and Chips have this amazing aroma all of their own and my stomach responds to the waft of the vinegary chips with a very audible growl.

"If you're hungry you can always have some of mine, "Nanna offers me and she holds out her plate towards me. "I'll never manage to eat all this in a month of Sundays."

It is crunch time for me…I have in my hand a plate with three crispbreads on it which, if I am really honest, actually DO taste like cardboard, never mind resembling it. And in front of me is the offer of food that feels like manna from heaven at that precise moment in time. Crispy, golden haddock…plump, oil-covered chips…there is no contest really. I am so very tempted.

But, NO!! I can't give in so soon and so easily. God, what kind of wimp AM I? The crispbreads here on my plate represent far more than food—they show the iron will and the steely control that I have got over my life right now. They are a symbol of the vast difference that I KNOW I can make to my entire life. If I give in now, then everyone will know that I am a total failure. They'll be able to see it in every extra ounce of flesh that I carry painfully around with me. I simply CANNOT give in…

But the chips look so lovely…just one or two maybe?

"Well? Do you want some or not?" Nanna persists. "I can't stand here all day whilst they get cold."

"NOT!" I almost shout at her and I turn on my heels and head up to my room as fast as I can, clutching my plate of crispbreads so tightly that my fingers turn bright red. Even when I have closed my bedroom door tightly behind me and laid my dressing gown along the crack at the bottom of the door, I can still smell that wonderful aroma of Fish and Chips sneaking into my room…

No, No…I must change the way I think about them now I am not allowed to eat them. The smell is sickly…there, that's better. They are oily, full of fat, disgusting, nauseous, foul, revolting…

The smell seems to be clinging to my clothes and my skin though, and it is even inside my nostrils so that I can barely breathe without almost tasting them. The smell is teasing me, tempting me still. It is almost a part of me and I want that food so damn badly I could cry…

It is pure mental torture but I force myself to sit down on my bed and very slowly I nibble round the edges of the crispbreads, taking as long as I possibly can to eat them. I need to make them last longer than the Fish and Chips that are being devoured downstairs. It seems incredibly important to me that I make my meal last a lot longer than theirs—almost as if it is a contest that I simply HAVE to win.

I am still nibbling at the last quarter of the very last crispbread when I suddenly hear footsteps on the stairs and Diane's voice says:

"We're all going for a walk now, down by the river. Do you want to come as well?"

I wolf down the last of my meal in a flash and grab my jacket from the back of the chair. A walk…that means I'll be using up plenty of extra calories, and also if I go out now, then I can avoid having my yoghurt which means I'll be having even less that I had planned to, which just HAS to be good, doesn't it?

Going down the stairs after Diane I feel a deep sense of satisfaction growing within me. I have faced up to this evil demon inside me and won hands down. I have stared temptation right in the face and have walked away unscathed. No one and nothing can make me eat something I don't want to now. *No one.*

I don't even notice the lingering smell of haddock and chips as I open the living room door. I am immune now…

Minus Fifteen Pounds…

Outside it is a beautiful sunny day, but here I am, shut away in my bedroom with the curtains closed against the golden light which is invading my head and reminding me that there is a normal life outside of these four walls. I am in utter turmoil right now and I pace up and down the small patch of pale green carpet beside my bed like a caged animal, trying desperately to think of a way out of this terrible situation.

You see, I had all my calories worked out precisely for today, as I always do. I am very rigid about that and up until now not one extra calorie has passed my lips. I have been so damned good at this. I work it all out the night before, down to the very last calorie in a glass of low calorie soda, and then I know exactly what I am allowed to eat. If I stick to the plan rigidly, I know I will be just fine and I can get through the day, whatever life throws at me.

Except today it all went horribly wrong and in the middle of the afternoon I was stupid enough to let down my guard and I had an extra apple…and it wasn't even a small one either. How could I have possibly allowed that to happen? I have risked everything, my happiness, and my sanity, for one bloody apple that I didn't even really want in the first place. It was just sitting there in the fruit bowl and as I walked past the table, I found myself reaching out and grabbing it. Before I was really aware of what I was doing I was half way through eating it.

There are forty extra calories in my stomach now, maybe even fifty, or perhaps sixty as it was such a big apple. Trust Nanna to buy the big ones this week. I am usually so good with my eating as well. How could I have slipped so very easily? I don't deserve to have sunshine in my room, I don't deserve a decent shot at life, I am so damned weak and greedy and disgusting. I need to make up for this right now before it is too late and I fall even further back to what I used to be. I need to punish myself somehow and make it all better again, but how?

I know—I'll go out for a walk. A LONG walk, and I'll make myself walk extra fast so that I am sure that I am burning off all those extra calories before they can have the chance to turn into yet more ugly fat on my body. I am only meant to have 500 calories a day now, according to my charts—if I have any more then I know for sure I will start piling back on all the weight I have successfully lost up to now and I just can't bear the thought of doing that. I'd rather die, I really would. Perhaps from now on I had better cut it down to 450 a day just to be on the safe side.

I get out all my calorie books and exercise charts and work out how long I will need to walk to burn off the calories in a very large apple, then I double it—no, I had better treble it just to make absolutely certain none of it is left in my system. I change into a sleeveless tee shirt and shorts, even though I am feeling a little chilly today despite the hot sun, because I know that if my body is cold it will use up even more calories, and then I set off to walk along the river.

After walking for around half an hour I start to feel sick, but no way will I let myself turn back. I have created this situation—now I must deal with it in the only way I know how and to hang with how I feel. It is my own fault. I must keep walking…left foot forward, right foot forward. I have to keep going until I feel safe again.

Two hours and twenty minutes later I am back at the house, totally exhausted, dehydrated, sunburned, and with blisters on both heels. My legs ache terribly, my shoulders are stinging with the heat and my feet are throbbing. I collapse into the nearest chair and try to close my eyes to the pain, which seems to fill every inch of my body. I feel terrible and am so glad that Nanna is out and that she isn't here to see the state I am in.

But, if I am totally honest with myself, just below the intense physical discomfort is that now familiar sense of satisfaction and pride in my own willpower. I have beaten 'it'—the demon, the tempter. I have beaten myself, and thank God I have done it as well. I vow to never make that same mistake again. Never will I eat one extra calorie more than I am allowed, I swear…

Minus Twenty Pounds…

Today is an absolutely fantastic day! I feel so focused, SO on track and REALLY pleased with myself. It is amazing! I am losing weight—I KNOW I am as the scales say so, even though I can't see it so well myself, but other people must be able to. They are looking at me differently now at school. They don't just ignore me or sneer at me as they walk past, but they look at me admiringly and comment on how well I am doing. I bet they never thought I would be strong enough to do this, did they? Fat old Nonentity that I was! Now I have shown them all. Now I AM somebody. Well, at least I am on my way to being somebody now. I still have such a long way to go yet and much more weight to lose before I'll be truly happy with myself and my life though.

Everyone is envious of me, you see, because they don't have as much willpower and self control as me. I can see it in their eyes. They all want what I have found but they can't have it—it is MINE and nobody on this earth can take it away from me. Gayle and Diane always try to get me to eat something extra when they come to visit now. It's like a game to them, tempting me with vile chocolate or disgusting cake, but I will NEVER give them the satisfaction of seeing me give in. It gives me such a buzz to look right at the food, say No and walk away triumphantly.

Nanna says I don't need to lose any more weight now, but I think she has always preferred me to be fat anyway, so she's bound to say that, isn't she? She says I should stop dieting now before I go too far but that would be a disaster. I have only got a fraction of the way towards being happy—how can I give up now? NO WAY!

I have found that I can weave just about every part of my life into my efforts to lose weight; it's just brilliant how I have adapted things to suit my purpose. I go to all the school discos I can now because dancing is such great exercise, and even when there are no discos to go to I can dance for hours to records in my room. I wake up with the alarm at six am every day and go out for a two-hour walk before getting ready for school, rain or shine. At school I have to sit down far too much in classes and this way I am at least getting a little exercise before I am made to rest. I hate resting. I do as little of it as I can. I would never sit down if I didn't have to.

The exercise routine I have made up is getting longer now and I sometimes do it three or four times a day, depending on how much I can fit in. I am even studying harder for my exams so that I can keep my mind off food. Mostly it works and when it doesn't I just take myself completely away from temptation and go for a walk.

I've started cooking meals for Nanna and Aunty as well, which I never used to do, as I get a real sense of pleasure from seeing other people eat what I prepare, all the while knowing full well that I am strong enough to avoid it altogether. I thrive on that feeling of power, and want it to last forever. It doesn't matter how hungry I am, I can always walk away from food now. I see anything which isn't on my chart as a kind of poison which mustn't invade my body or I will die. I WILL die as well, maybe not physically, but certainly spiritually. My entire being depends on avoiding that food at all costs. I am allowed my 400 calories a day and that is it, no more, but always less if I can manage it.

How very powerful I feel…and to think that not long ago I was so very weak-willed and had absolutely nothing in my life at all. I WAS nothing. But now…ah, losing even this small amount of weight has given me wings and I feel like flying…

Minus Twenty-Five Pounds...

Whatever I do, I can't seem to rid myself of these awful, gnawing hunger pangs today. They make my stomach churn and ache and whatever I try to do is overridden by this urge to eat and stop the pain. I have walked, I have danced, I have read, I have studied, I have watched TV, but everything seems to pale into the distance and all I can concentrate on is this excruciatingly empty feeling in my stomach.

I have had my tea early tonight as it is, in an attempt to curb the hunger but even that hasn't worked. I ate my can of garden peas very slowly, one by one on the end of my fork, and then I cut my pear into tiny little cubes to make it last longer, but I still felt as ravenous at the end of the meal as I did at the start. What on earth could be wrong with me today to make me feel so bad? And how am I going to get through the rest of the night feeling this way, without giving in to the temptation and having something else to eat? I have had all my allotted calories for the day. I simply CAN'T have any more...I would rather die than eat any extra...

But it hurts so very much right now...

Nanna asks me what is wrong and I just tell her that I have period pains which is an out and out lie as I haven't even had a period for about six weeks now. She grunts and says that maybe if I ate a little more then I wouldn't feel so bad and that I don't eat enough to keep a sparrow alive, which is one of her favourite sayings right now. But what does SHE know? She can never understand how I feel, and how very important it is to me NOT to eat.

"Have a sandwich, "she suggests. "Surely that won't hurt, will it?"

I just about laugh in her face. A sandwich?! Doesn't she realize what she is saying? There is no way on this earth I could eat all that—two whole slices of bread with margarine and a filling as well—that's like a whole days worth of calories all in one go, if not more!

But, despite my protests, the idea of the sandwich has taken actually root and is planted firmly in my head now. A Technicolor vision of it in all its glory swims around in front of my eyes as if it is torturing me. I want to reach out and grab it so much that I sit on my hands for fear that it is real and I will take hold of it and devour it before I can stop myself.

I stare fixedly at the television screen in front of me instead. Nanna is now watching some documentary about the Arctic and she is totally engrossed in it. She is completely unaware of the absolute power struggle that is taking place right now within my brain. I bet I don't even look any different to her, but inside I feel as if all my power and control are slipping away from me and I am slowly dying in front of her eyes without her even knowing.

If I make myself that sandwich now I will die, it is as simple as that. Everything I have fought for since this diet began will have been in vain—people will laugh at me again, I won't belong any more, I won't BE anything anymore, my life will be finished. This is my one last chance to make something of myself. I am sitting here fighting for my very existence whilst watching an advert for toothpaste…

In the end I decide to just go to bed early and try to sleep. There is no other place for me to go to be safe. I can never hide from myself, can I? I lay down and pull the covers right up over my head and cocoon myself under the blankets, with my knees drawn up over my aching stomach, and I cry myself softly to sleep.

Minus Thirty Pounds…

My exercise routine seems to be getting harder every day but I have to persist with it, no matter how badly I feel. If I missed even one day then everything would be spoilt and my whole world would disintegrate. My food intake, my weight, and my exercise regime are all that holds me together these days.

I do the self same exercises every single day for exactly the same length of time. I don't even have to think what to do now as I have a tape of songs that I have hand picked for their upbeat tempo and I just put it in the machine and off I go. The tape lasts exactly forty five minutes now—it used to be fifteen minutes when I first started dieting but I have built it up and will maybe even have to make it longer soon as I am sure it isn't working as much as it should be. Each of those minutes is spent in predetermined movements designed to stretch and tone and shrink every major muscle in my body and do away with every last inch of fat on my disgusting self.

Even before I do the first exercise today I can feel myself shaking. I have no energy some days and I know that my blood sugar can't be that high but there's nothing I can do about that. I am not scheduled to eat again for another two hours and after my evening meal I am always too tired to exercise so I have to do it right now, whether I feel up to it or not.

Ten minutes into the routine and a cold clamminess washes over my face.

I feel so faint and more than a little sick but I must keep going.

Twenty minutes and my bones ache and the shaking has worsened, making it more difficult than ever to move my limbs as I need to.

Thirty minutes and I am amazed that my legs haven't given way underneath me. I am willing them to hold me up for another fifteen minutes. I simply HAVE to finish this routine.

Forty-five minutes later and the last song finishes. I switch off the tape with tremendous relief and sink to my knees, shaking so badly that I am convinced I am going to pass out completely. I was prepared for this though. This isn't anything new to me as I feel like this most days now. Today is just a little worse than usual, that's all.

I reach out awkwardly for my glass of soda, low calorie of course, in fact only ONE calorie in the whole glass—I'm desperate for a drink after that work out. I manage to pour most of the fluid into my mouth, although a generous amount of it hits my tee shirt as well as I can't keep my hand still enough to hold the glass properly. I allow myself five minutes to sit completely still which is a luxury, just to let the shaking subside a little before I can continue with my day. I don't usually let myself sit down and rest, so I always feel terribly guilty on the rare occasions that I do. Five minutes on the dot and it is time to stand up again and study, with my books resting on the windowsill. Standing uses up far more calories than sitting down does, and if I rock backwards and forwards on my heels whilst I stand, then that uses up even more. I have it all worked out. There is no time to relax really, no time to stop; I HAVE to keep going…

I have to…

Minus Thirty-Five Pounds…

I can't get myself up out of bed today for some reason. My head is pounding, my limbs feel so weak and cold, and it is almost as if every last inch of my body feels sick. It is an awful feeling and one I can well do without today as I have so much to get through. So much planned. I have a stack of revision to do. My 'O' Level exams start in four weeks time and I simply have to pass them all and pass them well. Everyone expects me to do well and I can't let them down.

Nanna has let me shut myself away in her bedroom over the past few days so that I can concentrate properly without constantly being interrupted by

Aunty's children who are always in and out of my room. Some days I do up to eight hours revision at a time without even a break for food. Who needs food anyway? There are FAR more important things in life than eating.

Plus I have to do my exercises before I start revising. I can't miss a day of exercises, no matter how bad I feel or my muscles will turn straight back to fat again before I know it. Lying here in bed is useless to me as it barely uses up a single calorie and I feel so damn lazy. There's no way I can lie here all day, even though that is what my body is screaming at me to do. Well, tough…I have to get up.

Nanna comes into the room and say she will make me a cup of milky tea with sugar in it to give me some energy, or maybe a cup of hot chocolate. Never mind the calories for once, she tells me, they are only drinks after all, not food. But she doesn't understand that these drinks are just as evil as the food I avoid. They are laden with calories as well. I drink my tea and my coffee black these days—no milk, no sugar—so she should know better than to offer me something as repulsive as milky sugary tea. I feel nauseous even thinking about the damage a couple of spoons of poisonous sugar could do to my system.

I shake my head at her weakly and my vision blurs for a second or two and I am sure I am going to either be sick or pass out completely. But thankfully it passes.

"I'll just have a drink of water for now," I tell her and slowly I raise myself into a sitting position, breathing deeply to fight off the rising nausea in my stomach.

Nanna doesn't make a move. She looks so very sad and for a moment I think she is about to say something to me, but she must have thought better of it for she turns and leaves the room quietly. Can't she see that I am doing this for HER as well? To make her proud of me and all that I can achieve? I just want her to be happy for me and support me in what I am doing. After all I am doing so very well in my efforts to lose weight. I have lost thirty-five pounds now and I have only been dieting for two and a half months. That's not bad at all, is it? I know it should be more but I am doing okay really.

I have to lie back down again as the room is spinning around me and I feel as if I am going to faint right there and then. By the time Nanna comes back with my glass of water, I am asleep again…my eyes just won't stay open.

Minus Forty Pounds...

Being little means feeling safe.

It means that someone can easily wrap their arms around you and love you with all their heart and protect you at all times.

It means that you can hide away from the world more easily and nobody sees you as you walk down the street. You are so very small that people hardly notice you.

Being little means that I can curl up into a tiny ball and no one will be able to reach me or hurt me ever. I am little, I am anonymous and I am safe.

They keep asking me WHY...why am I doing this? Why don't I eat? Why am I starving myself? Why won't I accept any help or do as they want me to do? Can't they see? It is all perfectly crystal clear to me, but I can't even begin to explain it to them. It is simple though, and they should be able to see it if they only looked hard enough.

I want to be little again—NO, it's far more than that...I NEED to be little, and if I don't eat I will get smaller. It all makes perfect sense, doesn't it? And if I am smaller they will love me more—the way people are supposed to love and protect little children.

I can remember being little in such detail and I really yearn for those days, even though they weren't very happy days. I just loved being able to sit in a big grown-up chair and swing my feet back and forth, revelling in how far they were from the ground. It felt as if I were a princess up in a high tower, looking down to the ground and feeling so very safe. No one could possibly reach me up here. I hated it when I grew taller and my feet began to slowly touch the ground. I would push myself as far back in my chair as possible to try and make them swing as they had before, but there came a time when I was so big that there was no further back to go.

I hated this new connection I had with the world. It made me feel that I now had certain responsibilities, people had expectations of me, I was no longer the little princess sitting high up in her tower, safe and sound, oblivious to the adult conversations around me. Now they expected me to join in and be one of them. I felt ordinary somehow, like I no longer had a chance to be special to anyone ever again.

I loved being little and standing beside Granpa and not even being tall enough to reach his shoulders. He seemed so big and solid to me, and just being next to this obvious strength and seeing him tower above me made me feel as if nothing in this world would ever hurt me, ever. Of course it did,

THEY did, but being beside Granpa could make me forget that somehow.

As my height gradually crept up towards his, it was almost as if the balance of power shifted somehow. For every inch I grew I felt I should take on an inch more responsibility for caring for myself, protecting myself, standing on my own two feet, making my own decisions. But nobody had ever shown me how…

The fear of being bigger, being older would engulf me completely some days. I could never imagine myself standing alone. I could never take care of myself. I would never be safe enough. I didn't want to be an adult. I didn't want to grow up. I DON'T want to grow up. I want to be little…

And now, as I shrink physically, I feel as if I am shrinking in actual height as well, although I know that isn't actually possible. I know I have lost some weight, not that I can see it much—just the scales tell me so—but I know I have to lose a lot more before I am little enough. The numbers on the scale don't even mean too much to me right now. I will know inside me when I have reached my magic goal of being little enough. I am still far too big as I am; I can feel the fat on my bones, I can see it in the mirror. I repulse myself because I'm not yet the person I want to be. I need above all else in the world to be little.

I think of nothing else these days—just losing weight, getting smaller, and making my world perfect and safe. It's all I want in this world. If I can't be little, then I don't even want to BE…

Minus Forty-Five Pounds…

Let the Day Pass

Let the day pass by quickly, let the hours slip away.
Let night come and shelter me from this tortured day.
Let the troubles before me melt into the past.
How long can they plague me, how long can this last?

I'm sick and I'm frightened, I'm scared of the day,
I'm afraid of its problems, let them all fade away.
Will someone please take me away from this life,
Where the words that surround me don't cut like a knife.

Where each day that comes isn't marred by the pain,
And thoughts of the joy I may never regain.

So take this day from me and give me a night
Where rain turns to sunshine and darkness to light

I wrote this poem last night, just before I settled down to sleep, but heaven knows where those words came from, as my life couldn't be better right now! I look forward so much to going to school these days, just to hear all the fantastic things that people are saying about me, especially when they comment on how THIN I am! Can you believe that?? They are saying that *I* am thin!! Even Emma has stopped being such a cow to me and seems to look at me differently because I have lost weight.

I still think they're exaggerating a lot as I'm nowhere near being THIN, but it's great to hear them saying it anyway. I suppose I am thin-NER compared to the huge fat blob I used to be, and that is probably what they mean more than anything else. Besides, some of my school clothes are quite baggy now, as I can't afford to buy anything smaller at the moment. I feel really guilty asking Nanna to buy clothes for me, seeing as she bought me a whole new uniform just a few months ago and it isn't even worn much yet. I suppose that the baggy clothes I wear just now are bound to make me look thinner than I really am. I've still got a long long way to go though before I AM thin, and I mustn't get knocked off track by all these incredible compliments.

People who would never have given me the time of day when I was heavier now come up to me and ask how much weight I have lost and what diet I am on. I make things up about what I eat as it would sound so stupid if they knew I was living on three small tins of baby food a day now. Baby food is really lovely though and it makes perfect sense to me to eat it. It's not filled with too many calories as the tins are just little, and they MUST have all the right vitamins in them if they're for babies, right? So they must be really healthy to eat. Nanna thinks I am absolutely crazy now, but she still buys the tins for me when I ask her to. I suppose she is just glad that I'm eating fairly well and have given up eating the tins of peas and broad beans and that awful low calorie bread that I lived on for a month or so. Anyway, I tell the kids at school who ask, that I am following a thousand calorie a day diet plan that I found in a magazine somewhere. I make it as vague as possible so that I never have to give much away. No one must EVER know what I really do. It is all mine, after all…

Even Mrs. Bell, the really snooty English teacher, called me back after class today and asked how I was getting on as she could see that I had lost such a lot of weight and so very fast as well. I was really flattered when she said that. It's not often that a teacher takes such a personal interest in you, and she's only ever talked to me in class about work. She also went on to ask if I had any problems I would like to talk over with her and that if I did, she was always free at the end of the school day. She seems to think I am ill or something! But that couldn't be further from the truth! My life is better than it has EVER been!

I now have a path to follow and as long as I stick strictly to the rules of my new path then I will be just fine and I will always be okay. Sure it can be tough going at times—like last night when I must have been feeling low enough to write that poem—but nothing really worth having is going to come easy, is it? I simply know no better way to live right now. It's this way or no way at all. I can't go back to the way I was living before, so I have no choice, do I?

But I don't even want to think about the way life was before this life-saving diet began or else the gaping black hole comes back into my mind and the old familiar fear threatens to engulf me once more. So I push all these thoughts as far from my mind as I can and refuse to even contemplate not being able to live this way forever. I could never lose all this power and control now. It won't happen to me anyway. I have found the only way to live—and life is just wonderful. Why can't everyone else see that too and just be happy for me?

Minus Fifty Pounds…

I have dared to look at myself naked in Nanna's full-length mirror for the first time ever today and I am so shocked at what I see before me. I am still absolutely enormous, even after losing all this weight and I am utterly disgusted at all the excess fat I can still see spreading out across my bones. Not that I can even see my bones, of course. They are shrouded in all this repulsive fat.

But it's the strange bruises that shock me the most, if I am honest. I had never noticed them before today as I hardly ever look at my body, it shames me that much, but now I am amazed at just how many of these bruises I have got and in so many different places.

My hip bones are all purple and red—it can only be from lying flat on my stomach in bed at night because I certainly haven't done anything else to them. It is really sore to lie in any position in bed these days. I can never seem to get comfortable and my joints hurt a lot. I guess my hips DO jut forward just a little bit but there is still plenty of fat around them that I simply HAVE to get rid of before I can stop dieting. I'll just have to find another way to lie in bed, that's all.

There are even smaller bruises on my knees, and my elbows—they are on most of my joints in fact. I must be knocking myself a lot when I am exercising without realizing I am doing it. I certainly throw myself about enough to the music and sometimes I get a little dizzy and I fall down so that would explain some of the knocks. Oh well, what do a few bruises here and there matter anyway?

Nanna says I am all skin and bone right now which is a stupid saying anyway, as isn't everyone all skin and bone? What else are we made of if not that? I know that she really means I am too thin and bony but I just can't see it at all. If she could only look at me now the way I am seeing myself in this mirror, there is no way she would ever be able to say I was thin. Just look at me! All I can see is the skin, no bones—far too much skin all over me. There's nothing at all for her to worry about.

Anyway, the bruises will fade and nobody else will ever see them, not all of them, and they don't hurt that much so I shall just pretend that they're not there. I don't need to eat any extras, like Nanna says I do. I couldn't anyway, even if I tried. I think I would just throw up. Nanna has always tried to fatten me up, ever since I can remember—huge plates of food, enormous bowls of home made trifle—God, I used to be so disgusting with all that I crammed into my mouth. No wonder I was such a big fat pig.

No, I can't and I WON'T go back to that again, not even if Nanna begged me to. I couldn't be that person again, that huge Nothing, not to please anyone…

I get dressed quickly and vow to never look at myself again. Not if I can help it, anyway

The Outsider

I am standing at a mirror, looking right into myself,
Living a life that is not mine

And I wish that I could change so many things.
But mostly I feel powerless
Still knowing that this has got to be the time for change.

I join in the laughter of others,
When really I see nothing funny in their merriment
And I do as others do
So that I am not One Alone.
Too unsure of myself to BE myself
And too proud to be anyone else.

I am living my life from the outside.
A stranger in my own world
Waiting for someone to open the door
And let me in,
Or just searching in vain for the key...

Minus Fifty-Five Pounds...

Wow...I have just realized that I haven't had my period for four whole months. I hadn't even thought about it until today when we were talking about periods in class—only because we think Janet is pregnant and the conversation kind of went on from there. Fancy being pregnant at sixteen? My God, and I think *I* have problems...

I wonder why my periods have stopped though? Not that I miss them at all as I have always hated having them ever since they started, but I still wonder if there is anything wrong with my body. Maybe I have cancer or something? Maybe I have a big tumour growing in my stomach or my womb or my ovaries, or wherever it is that would stop me having periods. Maybe I should go to the doctor and get checked out...

On second thoughts, no, NO WAY!! He would just comment on my weight like everyone else is doing these days and try to make me eat more and I just can't risk that. I'll just wait and see what happens. Maybe this is normal with periods. Maybe they come and go throughout your life. They may just come back on their own. I wish I had somebody I could ask, someone I could trust. I wish I didn't have to worry about these kinds of things on my own.

Maybe I should get a book from the library and see what I can find out, but then again I couldn't face the embarrassment of having the librarian seeing me with a book like that. There is this part of me that doesn't feel remotely feminine and never has really. When you are fat, people never see you as being any sex at all—you are just a Thing, a sexless being. I feel as if I have no right at all to lay claim to anything that a normal girl of my age would experience. In fact I feel a real fake when the other girls talk about their bodies and going out with boys, or even makeup. Nanna hates me wearing makeup. She calls it my 'muck', so I always put it on when I am out of the house so as to avoid her disapproval. I have never had a proper boyfriend, no boys even look twice at me really because I am so fat, and I feel about as feminine as a sack of potatoes. No wonder my periods have disappeared.

I'll try to look on the bright side though, as much as I can. Who in their right mind wouldn't be glad to be free of their periods? They're horrible, messy things which are only useful if you want to have children and I most certainly won't be having children for a long long time, if ever. I mean, who would ever want to…you know…with ME?? Men like skinny women best, don't they? And I have a long way to go until I am anywhere near skinny. No one will ever want to come near me.

But then what if they DON'T come back and I can NEVER have children? That would be awful, if I never even had the chance. Or would it? Maybe not, now I come to think of it. At least I would never be able to do to my own children what was done to me, or what I saw done to others. I'd make an awful mother anyway—some people just aren't meant to be mothers, are they? I can't imagine ever having that responsibility. I'd be bound to screw up.

I begin to throw out the occasional sanitary towel so that Nanna doesn't suspect that I'm no longer having periods. I don't want her to start to hassle me about that too. I have enough to think about right now…

Minus Sixty Pounds…

I feel so very cold today and I am sitting here in class shivering, even though the sun is splitting the pavements outside. I just can't seem to get warm whatever I do. Maybe I am coming down with a bug or something.

It's July but I'm wearing my thick polo neck jumper and I've been getting some weird glances today. I know what the other kids think—most girls who wear polo neck jumpers at school when it is warm are covering up love bites and everyone must be wondering who on earth would be stupid or blind enough to give ME a love bite! They couldn't be more wrong if they tried!

I feel as if I stick out like a sore thumb in class today. Everyone else is wearing tee shirts or short sleeved blouses and here's me in my winter woollies. I wish I could just disappear into my chair, or better still just disappear completely and not even exist. Instead I sit here (and how I detest sitting down—what a waste of the calories I could be using up if I could stand up or walk about instead) and I shiver my way through another deathly boring History lesson. Why did I ever choose to do History anyway? The teachers are awful and the subject is so dry. Who needs to know about the Industrial revolution anyway? What good will it ever do us?

This morning before I put on my school uniform, I took another look at the soft downy hair that has been growing all over my body recently. It's been there for a few weeks, I suppose and even when I shave it off it keeps on coming right back. I am so afraid it will just keep growing and growing and never stop and I'll be even more of a freak than I already am. What on earth is wrong with me?

Then it clicks, as I am sitting there in History, not in the least bit concentrating on what Mr. P is saying. This must be my body's way of keeping itself warm as I continue to lose weight. I mean, I know I eat enough through the day, but with all the extra exercise I have been doing, maybe my body can't maintain its own heat quite the same. We've been doing about things like this in Biology and it never occurred to me until now that that must be what is happening to me. That would explain why I feel so cold as well. That must be it! Thank God for that!

I am quite relieved I have figured it out. After all, it's a good thing, isn't it? It means that my body is using up all the calories I am putting into it just fine—more than just fine really. I have 350 a day now, which still seems a lot to me and I know I should have less, but at least I know now that I have another way to use up more calories. I will wear a tee shirt to school tomorrow like the other girls do, and then I will be even colder and will use up even more calories! What a great idea! Anything—I would do anything at all if it meant I could use up more calories and lose more weight. I'll do whatever it takes to reach my goal of thinness…

I shiver again as a cool breeze comes in through the nearby open window, but now I am glad I am cold. There go a few more calories out of my system without me even trying…

Churning

Churning, always churning, these torments in my mind,
Decisions I should never have to take
Become the centre of my egotistic existence.

Should I feed my Devil
As he screams for more and more?
My resistance is not so strong these days
And I do not even know the reasons why.

My mirror is distorted too
As my mind goes round and round.
The shape I see grows out of all proportion
Until I see the picture
That is in my devil's eye.

Inside my head I'm screaming,
For nobody can ever know
The fear, the confusion, the hate and shame I feel
As I watch myself slipping
Further down every day.

And every day is just like that last
An endless chain...? But NO!
Not endless for I know one day I will conquer
This indefinable evil
Which is so much a part of my life today
And I'll live at last as me alone.
Just me alone,
Just ME...

Minus Sixty-Five Pounds...

I read a magazine article today about a girl who has this disease called Anorexia Nervosa and it has really got me thinking. So I decide to go to the library to see if I can find out more about it. But I can't just go to the local library like normal people, can I? Oh, no, nothing is ever as simple as that these days. I have to walk nine miles to a different library just so that I can be sure I get enough exercise for the day. I can always catch the bus back home if I am tired, except that I know there is no way I would do that. I'd have to sit down if I caught the bus, wouldn't I, and I'm not allowed to sit down again until tea time.

The walk isn't too bad, except that I have to stop a few times along the way as I feel dizzy and I'm afraid I will fall into the traffic that is whizzing past my side. There are no proper pavements on these small country roads and I have to be extra careful, but I make it to the next town okay without being mown down! Just!

The reference section of this library is huge and it takes me quite a while to find the books that I need. I carry them back to a table and stand there flicking through the pages until I find what I want and then I start to read and make notes. Several phrases jump right off the page at me straight away;

"self induced weight loss through extreme dieting, loss of monthly periods, marked concern about food and eating."

Okay, well, I suppose that would describe me a little bit. What else is there?

"sufferers are predominantly young women, they may use excess exercising, self induced vomiting, laxative or diuretic abuse to lose weight"

Ah, well the only bit that applies to me there is the bit about exercise, as I have never done anything else like made myself sick or taken laxatives, so I can't really be anorexic if I only have SOME of the symptoms, can I? Then I see a section entitled "Causes of the Disorder" and I read on. This should be interesting.

"social pressure, a genetic predisposition, a personality characterized by conscientiousness and striving for high achievement"

Hmm…I don't know about that. Maybe a little bit like me but not enough to make me worry. Let's see what the treatment is next.

"The initial phase of treatment focuses on restoring weight."

I slam the book shut with such a bang that I get some very frosty looks from the librarian and the other people in the library. I hastily put all the books back on the shelves, as I don't need to know any more AT ALL. These symptoms don't describe me in any way and I am NOT anorexic. No way do I need to have my weight restored. I am NOT anorexic.

I walk out of the library and find myself right opposite the bus stop. The bus back to my house is due in ten minutes and I have plenty of money in my purse for my bus fare home. My feet are already sore from the walk here and my back is aching too. Maybe I should just get the bus after all.

I turn around though and begin the nine-mile walk back home. I can't afford to sit down for that length of time. I have to walk.

Every single step of the journey home I tell myself I am NOT anorexic, I am NOT anorexic…I am NOT…

Minus Seventy Pounds…

This has been the most unbelievable day of my life and I still can't believe that it has happened. I can't believe I have let myself down so very badly and ruined all I have achieved so far. I know I will pay for this huge mistake in a big big way.

What happened to me? Why did I do it? I just can't figure it out at all. It makes no sense to me and my head is spinning frantically, trying to cope with what I have done to myself.

It is just another normal day; nothing out of the ordinary at all. It is a Sunday in August and I am working at my weekend job at the newsagents' shop two miles away from home as I usually do. I have worked here for a few weeks now and I quite like the job. Okay, so I am surrounded by chocolate bars, jars of sweets, and boxes of chocolates all day long, but it doesn't phase me at all as I have trained myself to shut these objects out of my mind almost as if they were alien to me, which I suppose they are after all this time. At the end of every Sunday shift I buy a small selection of sweets to take home for Nanna, Aunty and the two children; just little penny sweets as a treat for them and this day is no different.

I always walk to and from the newsagent's (of course) and today on the way home I suddenly find myself dipping into the bag of liquorice sweets I have bought for Nanna. It is crazy as I don't even like liquorice and never have, but before I know it I am pushing them into my mouth and devouring them so fast I can hardly taste them anyway. I begin to shake at the enormity of what I have just done. The whole bag of sweets has gone now, I can't believe I have eaten a whole bag of sweets—me, who wouldn't even have an extra drink of one-cal yesterday as it would have taken me over my limit. NOW look at me.

I promise myself that when I get home I will stick my fingers down my throat and not give up until I have got rid of every last piece of those poisonous sweets. I almost run home in my desperation to rid myself of this excess food as quickly as I possibly can. I feel as if it is killing me from the inside out, and I need to get it out of me fast.

It's not as easy as I thought it would be though. No matter how much I try and try to be sick, I just can't seem to do it, and all I can manage is an eye watering bout of retching which turns me bright red and has Nanna knocking at the bathroom door, wanting to know if I am okay.

"I'm fine, I'm fine, "I shout to her and I wait until she has gone back downstairs before I try again. But it is no use. Maybe the sweets have gone too far down by now to be brought up again? What can I do? I can't just leave things like this with those sweets still inside me! Maybe if I ate a little more, and made myself so full that I actually WAS sick naturally? Would that work? What if it didn't and all the food just stayed there? God, what do I do?? Help me, help me out of this nightmare...Why, oh why, did I eat those damned sweets?

I choose to eat...and eat...and eat some more. I simply cannot stop now, even if I wanted to. Nanna looks at me, totally bemused by this sudden about turn in my behaviour, but she says nothing, as she must be so pleased to see me eat. I hate it that she is happy about this as it is an utter nightmare for me and I just want her to go away and stop watching me with that look of absolute glee in her eyes. This is disgusting—*I* am disgusting. I don't want anyone to see me at all.

I start off with a cup of tea –with plenty of milk in, something I haven't had since the start of this diet. I have six biscuits from the tin that I haven't been near for months, then I have another six and dip them into my tea. Then I have a bar of chocolate that I brought home for the kids, who are out for a walk right now. Then I have two cans of my baby food, two sandwiches crammed full of ham and vegetable salad that tastes so incredibly creamy I want it to last forever. I find a bag of crisps, another bar of chocolate, devour them and then make myself a fresh cup of tea.

I feel absolutely and utterly out of control and I can almost watch myself from the outside as I carry on just eating and eating in this manic way. It feels as if I am being driven by some kind of demon and I have no idea how to make it stop. I am terrified, I feel like I am teetering on madness, and yet Nanna is looking on so relieved that I am actually eating. It is surreal. It is like the worst dream I could ever have imagined for myself but I am living it out and wishing I were dead rather than playing this nightmare of a role.

I eat more, and more, and then I stop, promising myself that this will be the last thing I eat for days and that NOW I will be sick. I feel so very ill that I can hardly move. My stomach is bloated and painful and fit to burst with all this unwelcome food. I can almost feel the calories, the thousands of calories draining into my system and I wish I could rip the food out of myself, it feels so alien inside me. I just have to be sick this time.

But it is no use. STILL it doesn't work. WHY can't I be sick? What do I have to do to make it happen? I can't fit anything else into my body yet I simply HAVE to be sick. I am so desperate now that I drink a glass of salt water even though it is disgusting. I simply cannot leave all this food inside of me to turn into fat and make me huge again. I can't live that way anymore. I will lose myself completely if I put on weight again. I will cease to be. I can't let that happen. Not again. I can't go back to that. It was no way to live, no way at all…

I put my fingers down my throat again…nothing. I sink down on my knees until I am lying on the bathroom floor and I pray that I will never get up again. I just lie there for ages; I really don't care how long I am there. After all, what is the point of standing up and using up more calories now? I have ruined it all.

In the space of one afternoon—no, just a few moments—I have become an entirely different person. This morning I was still ME, I was in control, I had a plan for the day, I was strong, I knew how to live, I knew what rules I had to follow and that I was okay. And NOW look at me! I am a wreck, I am weak, greedy, ugly, fat, disgusting, and useless…I hate myself more than I have ever hated myself in my whole life. I hate myself with such a passion that I want to die there and then on that bathroom floor. I really really want to die…

I can't believe that my whole world has turned upside down because of some awful liquorice sweets, which I would never ever have chosen to eat, even if I were able to have any food in the whole world. I HATE liquorice, so why did it prove to be my downfall?

I vow that for the next seven days I will eat only 100 calories each day and no more to make up for this atrocious landslide. I MUST get back on track. I can't let this affect my plans. I have so far to go, so much more weight to lose…

******

The next day I starve completely and only drink water until ten pm at night. I walk and walk all day. I feel nauseous and weak and I shake like a leaf but I walk and walk because I have to burn off some of the calories from yesterday and I can't allow myself to stop. I have to be punished for the wrong I have done. I try to work out just how many calories I ate yesterday and it is a terrifying number. It seems so huge and such an insurmountable task to use them all up again. It will take me days. I feel a crushing sense of defeat before I have even started, as if I am running from this giant tidal wave which is about to engulf me and it simply doesn't matter how fast I run, I cannot escape it.

That night, at ten pm, I open up a packet of biscuits that I find beside the tin, take them up to my room with a cup of tea and then I post them like letters into my mouth one by one until there are none left. My mind feels numb, my body aches and is weak and I wish I were anyone but me...anywhere but here in my life.

Looking Back...

During the six-month period that I was anorexic there was no room in my mind for casual thoughts, for pondering the world around me, thinking about boys, make up, clothes or whatever else sixteen-year-old girls had on their minds at that time. All I knew for sure, back then was that I HAD to be thin above all else, and I really didn't consciously think too much deeper than that. Every aspect of my daily life was just too overwhelming for me to deal with upfront. I had a poor relationship with my Nanna: I was living under unbelievably stressful conditions in an overcrowded house with two adults who seemingly hated each other, I was under pressure at school to get good results in all my exams, and I had weight problems which set me aside from all the other girls. I seemed to live in constant fear—fear of *what* I didn't really know at the time, but I was afraid every single day of my life. Focusing 100% on losing weight gave me leave to put aside every other problem in my life and deal solely with this one enormous situation.

Everything else in my life narrowed down and became part of this one desperately important goal of mine. People now talked to me because I was slimmer, when they had previously ignored me or looked at me as if I was something unsavoury they had just stood in by mistake. I got so much attention because I had lost a tremendous amount of weight so quickly and I was unused to even being noticed.

If life at home became too tough for me to handle, I could always hide away in Nanna's bedroom on the pretext that I was studying or avoiding food rather than face up to the fact that I just wanted out of this awful home environment. If the outside world invaded my mind too much and the fears swept over me like a tidal wave, I could simply make myself a new chart and work out how many calories I could have the next day. Or I could make up new menus for myself, new exercise routines—anything to cushion me against the perceived terrors of the world.

Starvation was an incredible emotional crutch for me at a point in my life where I felt that everything else was crumbling around me and I was losing what remained of my already fragile self amongst the chaos. It was the only foundation I had back then; my only way forward, and I clung to it desperately like a drowning man to a lifebelt. Anorexia WAS my lifebelt. Without it I would have died...maybe not physically, but certainly emotionally and spiritually.

Prior to the anorexia taking such a hold on me, I had felt totally out of control and terribly unsafe. There had been nothing in my life that I could securely hold onto, no firm foundations, nothing I could call mine, nothing to make me feel as if I even existed as a solid person. I did indeed feel like a 'Nonentity'. So, controlling my food intake in such a rigid fashion was the only aspect of my life that could be totally MINE—it was something that nobody else could take away from me, and I didn't want or need to share it with anyone else. Nobody could get inside my head; nobody could steal this control and this feeling of security away from me. I was safe. I was going to hang on to this feeling for all I was worth.

Anorexia was also a real cry for attention, but it was paradoxically a way of building a protective a wall around myself so that nobody could get in and hurt me any more. It was an attempt to stay small and childlike in order to avoid the pressures and responsibilities of adult life. But at the same time I was actively pushing people away from me and insisting that I was independent and could manage just fine by myself. Really, I had no idea what was going on. I was clutching at straws and living a frantic day to day existence which I saw as the only way out of the madness in my head.

I so much wanted those people close to me to understand what I was going through, especially Nanna, but no way would I give them any clues as to what was going on inside my head. I wanted to let them in but was terrified to let down my guard in case I lost any of my precious control over my eating and therefore my life.

I was starving every single day, desperate to eat but I would never allow myself to give in to hunger. I forced myself to see food as the 'evil enemy', which would consume ME, if I gave in to it, rather than the other way around. I thought I was focused and clear about what I had to do in life in order to BE somebody and avoid failure at all costs, but I was actually an out and out screwed up mess.

I thought I had found a wonderful strategy for coping with life and that I could live this way for ever, but in reality I was clinging onto a road that would have led me to a certain death had I not jumped off or fallen off as I did. I was dying slowly day by day, killing myself quietly, but I was still convinced that I had found a foolproof way to live. I thought it was ME who was in control but I was simply a vulnerable puppet, a slave to my illness, a victim of a harsh and unyielding master.

I believed I had found freedom, but I was to spend the next twenty years or more of my life shackled in chains…

Chapter Three

And So I Eat...

Plus Five Pounds...

This morning I wake up feeling terrible, both physically and mentally, and all I want is to turn over again and go right back into the blissful oblivion of sleep. But my mind won't let me. It is on fast forward as soon as I wake and it feels as if I have a loud, static-filled tape playing in my head that I have no control over at all. Words that I am not even conscious of thinking play over and over in my brain and I am forced to wake up much too soon.

I struggle to sit up in bed and then sink back down again as I recall the excesses of the previous night. My body is so hot and sick and bloated and my mind craves even more sugar the minute I am half-conscious. I vow that TODAY I will begin my diet all over again, TODAY is a brand-new day, and I reach awkwardly for the pen and paper beside my bed and begin to scribble down a whole new food chart for the day:

Breakfast: black coffee
Lunch: small apple, low calorie yoghurt, water
Tea: low calorie soup, orange, black tea
Supper: Pear (or nothing if I can manage it)

There is more than enough food there for me, isn't there? After all I used to survive on much less some days, and if I can only just manage ONE day like this, I am sure that I'll soon be able to get back on track again with my diet. I need to do it so very much...

It is five days since I abandoned my diet and turned into some kind of never-ending eating machine. These past few days have taken on a pattern of their own and I feel as if I have been thrown into someone else's life altogether. I haven't been able to stop eating at all, no matter how hard I try and it has been an absolute nightmare. I wish I could wake up one day and find out that I WAS someone else, but each day I look in the mirror and I am still me…more's the pity.

Today I have arranged to go swimming with Gayle and Diane and so I set off after my coffee and walk the two miles through the country to Mum's house. There is no sign of Alan today, thank goodness. I couldn't cope with HIM today and all his sarcastic remarks. He doesn't get to me as much as he used to these days because I have learned to answer him back, which he hates. He really doesn't like losing his almighty control over any of us, and so he takes every opportunity to put me down or embarrass me. I wish he would just disappear for good—I can never forget what he did.

Anyway, Gayle and Diane and I walk along to the nearby Sports Centre for our morning swim. I intend to get as much exercise as I can every day and so swimming is going to be a daily occurrence as long as I can afford to do it. I have such a lot of ground to make up and such a lot of weight still to lose, especially since I have been eating so much lately. It seems like an almighty steep hill to climb but I am determined to do it…

******

We have been swimming for about twenty minutes—well, to be honest, only *I* have been swimming properly. I am doing lengths up and down the pool whilst Gayle and Diane play with a beach ball at the shallow end. I feel kind of tired today but I won't let myself stop until I have done at least fifty lengths, however long it takes me. That is the goal I have set for today, and nothing less will do.

But…

I am nearly at the end of my twenty-third length, just approaching the deep end of the pool when suddenly my whole body seems to freeze and all the energy just drains sharply from every last part of me. It is as if I have lost the power in every single muscle I possess, and I feel as if I am going to pass out there and then. My head starts to spin, my vision clouds over and I try in vain to move my arms against the water to haul myself back to the side of the pool. At the very least I must try to reach somewhere I can put my feet on the bottom, but I just can't move at all. I am paralysed. What the hell is going on here?

Then…

As if in slow motion, I find myself sinking beneath the clear blue water and I can't breathe at all. It's as if a magnet is pulling me slowly towards the bottom of the pool and I haven't an inch of strength in me to fight it. I open my eyes but I can't see a thing and the chlorine in the water stabs at my eyes. I gasp for air and my lungs gulp in a mouthful of water and it feels like two very strong arms are wrapped around my chest, trying to squeeze the life out of me. I can't breathe, I can't move, I can't help myself. I am sinking further and further down into the pool and there seems to be nothing I can do to save myself at all.

Nothing…

This can't be real. Why isn't anyone coming to save me? There are three lifeguards on duty at this pool right now, there are at least forty swimmers in the water—how can I possibly be drowning in front of their eyes and yet nobody is coming to help me? People are even swimming past me, up and down the pool doing their lengths. Their limbs brush past me as they go by. Why won't they help? Is this even happening? Am I dreaming it all?

Help me…

There is water in my mouth, up my nose, in my lungs, everywhere, and I am desperate for some air. I keep gasping as if it will magically appear but I just take in more of this awful chlorinated water. I am drowning, dying, and there is absolutely nothing that I can do to save myself, as my limbs are still totally paralysed. I can feel myself losing consciousness and I am struck by the ridiculousness of this whole incredible situation. No way can my life end as stupidly as this! No way am I going to die in a swimming pool full of people who can't even seem to see me…

I can't die this way…

A sudden strength and determination hurtles through me at the very moment I think that, and just at the point where I feel I am going to pass out altogether, I find I can move my arms at last. Thank God!! I start to thrash about wildly until I begin to float further up in the water again and soon I have my face back into the air. I wave my arms around, trying to get my bearings in the pool as I take in huge lungs full of air. The breath flooding into my lungs feel like heaven and I take in as much air as I can until I feel alive again and the blood starts to flow around my body once more. I look frantically around and find Gayle and Diane hanging on to the bar around the edge of the pool. I can't believe it—they have spotted me, too, and they are simply waving at me and smiling! Don't they know what has just happened to me? This is surreal…Did it really happen? Did I imagine it? Surely not…

Heaven knows how but I find the strength to make my way back to the side of the pool and to safety. I don't know where that surge of energy comes from at all, or what caused me to almost black out in the first place, but none of that matters right now. I am safe again. One of the lifeguards has been looking on (looking on???!!!!) as I struggled back across the pool and he reaches down now to pull me up out of the water.

"What happened back there?" he asks me, wrapping a towel around my shoulders and guiding me to a chair in a small room by the pool. I am shaking like a leaf now and I can barely speak as my teeth chatter and my whole being shudders. I must still be in shock. Gayle and Diane have climbed out of the pool too, and at last they seem to have figured out that something was wrong. I am aware that there is another lifeguard with us now and I look up sharply as I recognise a familiar voice. It's Amanda from the same year as me at school—God, how embarrassing. Now everyone in the whole school will know about this. What is she saying now? I hear the word 'diet' being mentioned. What on earth is she telling him?

"She been practically starving herself for ages," Amanda is saying. "No wonder she passed out. Look how skinny she is."

I want to get dressed and get out of there fast, but first I have to sit through a totally humiliating lecture from the manager of the Sports centre about taking unnecessary risks by exercising whilst in an unfit state. What's more, it appears I was also putting other people at risk, namely his precious lifeguards—I would have laughed in his face if I'd had enough energy or nerve. The only risk *they* took was in getting their shoes splashed as they dragged me out from their position of safety at the poolside. They were no help to me at all.

But right then I can't even summon up the energy to talk to him and at last I am 'released' and allowed to go home. Mum isn't in when we get back and so I tell Gayle and Diane that I am walking back home and set off before they can begin to talk me out of it. I am like a zombie and I simply put one foot in front of the other and somehow make it home without collapsing.

******

I am lying on my bed, almost sleeping when Nanna storms into my room, obviously in quite a rage about something.

"And just when were you going to tell me that you nearly drowned today?" she shouts at me. "Funny how you didn't mention that when you came in. What the hell happened?"

Mum has been on the phone to see how I was—Gayle and Diane told her, of course. Nanna is furious. She has had ENOUGH of this damned slimming lark, she tells me. I am to get myself downstairs this minute and get some proper food inside me before I do myself some REAL damage. How can I do this to her?

Food…I haven't eaten at all today and I simply can't face the apple and the yoghurt that is on my chart for lunch. I need something warm and comforting and filling to make me feel safe again after such an awful day. I don't utter a single word of protest when Nanna places a plateful of sausages, creamy potato, and peas in front of me, followed by a large helping of sponge cake and custard. I just can't fight any more today. I have nothing left in me to fight with.

But tomorrow…yes, tomorrow is a new day, a fresh start, and I can begin my diet all over again. But just for today, I will eat…

Plus Ten Pounds…

A week or so after my escapade in the swimming pool Nanna and I are waiting at the bus stop to catch the ten o'clock bus into the town to do some clothes shopping. We are going on holiday tomorrow for a week to a guesthouse up in the Lake District and we're both really looking forward to getting away from everything here. With the increased tension at home of late we really need a change of scenery and I am quite excited about the prospect of lots of long walks and a chance to start a diet afresh in whole new surroundings. Perhaps this is just the impetus I need. God, I hope so.

I didn't feel too good first thing this morning though and this shopping trip very nearly didn't happen. My stomach was so very upset and I thought I was actually going to pass out as I sat doubled over in agony there in the bathroom. The pain in my stomach was incredible, although it was no surprise to me really, after the amount of food I had stuffed into myself last night. I deserved every last second of this pain for being such an absolute weak-willed pig and that self-satisfied thought made all the suffering just a little more bearable.

Anyway, the bout of illness had passed after a while and here we are now, waiting for the bus which is late as always. Nanna is telling me about the train we have to catch in the morning and how early we'll need to be up and I start to wonder why her voice is suddenly getting quieter, as if she is talking to me from quite a distance instead of standing right beside me. There are funny little specks dancing round in front of my eyes too, and I reach back clumsily to hold onto the fence of the house behind me. Something is wrong here…I feel so…so…

******

...And now I am lying on a sofa somewhere but I don't recognise the walls around me at all, nor do I recognise the woman's voice that is speaking in the background.

"Yes, that's correct. Number 26. Thank you. Goodbye."

There is a pause then:

"Don't worry, dear. The ambulance is on its way."

Ambulance? Am I dreaming? What is happening here? And then I hear Nanna's voice too.

"She's been dieting far too much...for months now...lost too much weight...too thin...nearly drowned at the swimming pool last week...no wonder she collapsed today..."

Collapsed...oh, boy. So that's what happened. No one has seen me open my eyes a little so I close them again quickly and try to fall back into that blissful unconsciousness.

The ambulance men have other ideas though when they arrive and they shout into my face to get me to wake up and talk to them. But I don't want to talk. I don't want to be. I imagine myself just fading away as I lie there, and if I open my eyes, then the spell will be broken somehow. One of the men lifts up my eyelid and I can't help but look at him, so he knows I am faking. Damn...

"She's okay," he grunts. "Come on, let's get her to the hospital and they can sort her out there."

What a fool I feel...They talk to me, ABOUT me, as if I am a stupid little kid.

Which is actually just how I feel at this moment in time...

******

So now I am up at the hospital and I feel like such a damn fraud. There is absolutely nothing wrong with me after all. I just had an upset stomach; I felt a bit faint, that's all. Why are they making such a big fuss of all this? Poor Nanna looks so small and so very scared as she sits beside the trolley I am lying on, whilst I wait to see the doctor. I want to reach right out and hug her but a huge wall of guilt holds me back and I lie there rigid and silent. It is all my fault this has happened. *I* have made her worry this way. I should never have given in to the food.

Everyone here has got it all so very wrong, though. I didn't collapse because I was *starving* myself—quite the opposite in fact. I collapsed because I am eating and eating as if there is no tomorrow, every day without fail, even though I promise myself at the start of each day that THIS day is going to be different. TODAY I will start again, and I always do—start, that is. Every day I start with the greatest of intentions but they never last for long. Maybe a morning, or until teatime if I am lucky. The longed for diet always turns into yet another day of me bingeing as if my life depends on it. I am far too ashamed to ever admit this to anyone though, and even Nanna doesn't know the full extent of my overeating, so it is far easier for me to let them believe I have ended up in hospital because I haven't eaten enough. Chance would be a fine thing though…

It is all very farcical really. After the doctor checks me over and barely speaks to me, I am allocated a bed in a woman's medical ward. They send a woman psychiatrist along to see me who asks lots of strange questions about my family life and my past. Silly questions like, Was Granpa a big man? Did I feel threatened by his size? How did I get on with my Mum…things like that. I can almost guess what she is trying to make me say so I give out what I think are the right answers and she goes away after an hour with heaven knows what written on her report about me. Psycho, no doubt! Who cares? Just get me out of here, fast! I'll say all the right things as long as I can go home where I am safe.

But I have to stay in overnight as I have a slight temperature and they want to make sure I will eat properly. Well, there are certainly no problems there, for sure. I eat all of my rotten hospital food, I eat a whole box of Maltesters that an old lady in the next bed gives me and I eat a big bar of chocolate that Nanna has bought me from the hospital shop downstairs. I would have had more if I'd had it there in front of me, but I ran out of supplies. They needn't worry about ME eating. It's *stopping* me eating that's the problem now, it seems. But the only person who sees this as a problem is me. The doctors, the nurses, Nanna, they all beam when they see I have eaten and then they make sure I haven't thrown it up some place. I feel like a puppy being patted on the head for performing a new trick...

"What a good girl, look how much you've eaten! Well done!"

******

The next day after tea I am allowed to go home as my temperature has dropped and they are satisfied that I am not going to starve to death over night. We should have gone on our holiday to the Lake District today, Nanna and I, but she had to phone up and postpone it for a week. We were lucky to still get into the same guesthouse as it was fully booked but there was a last minute cancellation. Well, at least there will still be plenty of long walks and that much needed chance of scenery, and that chance to start again. Thank God.

Nanna keeps on drumming it into me that this dieting has to stop for good now. Haven't I had enough warning signs, she asks me? I say the right things to her as well as I don't want her to worry about me anymore, but already in my mind I am writing out my next food chart. There is just no other way for me to live.

I have been given a letter by the hospital to take to my doctor and on the bottom of it is scrawled this priceless bit of medical advice for the future;

"Avoid strict slimming."

Amazing, isn't it? This patient has been starving herself for months, so what advice shall we give her?? Oh, I know—DON'T!! My faith in the medical profession goes down a notch or two right there and then. They tell me not to do it again but they never even asked me why I did it in the first place...

Nanna is going to make sure that I stick to this wonderful advice to a T though, as she is convinced that it was the so-called 'slimming' that got me into 'that state' in the first place and no matter what I say, nothing changes her mind on that score. But she is so very wrong...

Slimming, dieting, losing weight, whatever you want to call it, was never the problem. In fact, it was always the answer and always will be. If I hadn't gone off my diet in the first place, I would still be just fine. NO, it was, is and for ever more shall be the EATING that is the problem and if I don't sort that out very soon, then everything will be in ruins. There is still time to make it all okay again, but I have to start TODAY!!!

Plus Twenty Pounds...

The school bell rings for the end of the day and I am up out of my seat like a shot, out of the door and away before anyone gets a chance to hold me up. I hear Mary calling my name but I pretend I haven't heard her and I forge on ahead through the growing crowds of schoolchildren. I simply can't walk home with anyone today as what I am about to do needs no witnesses.

From the very moment I got up I have been planning this binge. Oh, I had a few 'good' moments when I first woke up when I was determined yet AGAIN that today was going to be the day I went back on my diet. Today would be the day that I rediscovered that immense control and got back on track. And those positive thoughts did indeed last—until I got out of bed, that is, and went downstairs and my eyes fixed immediately on the biscuit tin as if they were drawn to it by some kind of magnetic force. Instantly all my good intentions evaporated and, as if I had never ever been the person who could live quite happily on 300 calories a day, I grabbed a handful and ate them quickly before Nanna got up. At times like that I feel as if I am acting on automatic pilot. It isn't me who reaches for those biscuits. In fact all the while I am doing it, a terrified voice is screaming inside my head…NO! NO…but it makes no difference and I do it anyway. I feel as if I am going crazy here…maybe I am?

So from that moment onwards, I have planned an enormous binge for this afternoon after school. A huge final fling. Everything I love, everything I used to crave, so that I can get this tremendous urge to overeat out of my system once and for all, and then tomorrow I can start all over again, and be the ME I am supposed to be.

It takes me all of ten minutes to walk down the hill to The Square where all the shops are nestled together around the bus shelter and the car park, and I begin my 'mission'.

First I go to the bakers where I buy one vanilla slice, one individual fruit pie and two cream scones…

Next is the newsagents for one Mars Bar, one Twix, and a quarter pound of fudge…

Next the supermarket for a packet of custard cream biscuits, a trifle (family size, of course) and a raspberry sponge cake…

Then, grabbing tightly onto the carrier bags I am gathering, I cross the road to the bakers on the other side of The Square where I buy yet another vanilla slice (my favourite) and a large apple pie.

Finally, I go into the corner shop on the edge of The Square for my last purchase—a packet of chocolate digestive biscuits and a large fruit loaf.

I never buy too many items from one single shop for fear of arousing suspicion. I could never bear it if anyone even suspected that all of this food was for me. I act like a guilty shoplifter as it is, averting my eyes from the person at the check out as if I am trying to hide my guilty secret—which of course, I am. I want to shout out loudly that I am buying all this food for the family, for us ALL to eat, no big deal, it's not all for me, *honest!!* And I think I even begin to believe that myself as I add the last couple of items to my now bulging bags.

I feel as if I have committed some ungodly sin as I make my way home again through the crowds of after school shoppers. My palms are sweating, and my heart is pounding so loudly that I wonder if the people around me can hear it too. I keep bumping into people and stuttering apologies at them because I am in such a hurry to get home and begin the onslaught on the food. I'll have the whole house to myself for nearly an hour as Aunty and the kids are out for the day and Nanna goes to visit her friend every Tuesday afternoon until about half past five. I have about ninety minutes to eat all this food and there hasn't to be a trace of it left when anyone comes home. Every last crumb must be gone by half past five.

Being alone in the house is such a rare occurrence these days that I am excited about that in itself. I'll be able to sit downstairs in the warmth and have my binge instead of having to sneak the food up to my icebox of a bedroom as I usually do. Of course, I'll still have to keep a close eye on the time and keep an ear cocked for Nanna or anyone coming down the path just in case they are home earlier than expected. And I'll have to make sure I dispose of all the wrappers as I go along, as I would die if anyone found even one shred of evidence. But oh, it will be SO good—like being in heaven, safe and warm and full…

I reach the house and am so uptight and desperate to begin eating that I can hardly fit the key in the lock. My hands are trembling and I drop the key twice and have to take several deep breaths to calm myself down before I can finally get inside. Thank goodness no one is there. I had this terrible notion that everyone would have changed their plans at the last minute and God knows what I would have done then, but, no—the house is blissfully empty.

I fling my coat and schoolbag onto the nearest chair and rush into the warmth of the living room with my carrier bags of goodies, and then I set all the food out in front of me in the order that I want to eat it. It has to be eaten in a strict order, you see, or else the binge won't be 'right' and I may well have to do it all over again and I just couldn't face that. If I do even one thing wrong at this moment…well, I CAN'T…that's all. This is too damned important.

I arrange the softer foods first—the trifle, the sponge cakes, and so on.

Then next in line I have the apple pie and vanilla slices, the chocolate and sweets, etc.

Finally I will have all the biscuits which I'll dip into a mug of hot tea to soften them up and make them all smooth and creamy in my mouth. So, so comforting. Like being a baby all over again…I can hardly wait.

My food is all lined up in a row now and I frantically tear into the first item—the trifle—which bursts onto my tongue with all its wonderful flavours and textures, and gives me an instant fix—a high which compares to nothing I have ever felt. It shoots through every taste bud, and energises every nerve ending in my body, whilst at the very same time relaxing me and soothing my very soul. All is well in my world right now. Everything feels safe. I am home…

Right here, right now, this is the only place I am meant to be and nothing else in the entire Universe can make me feel this way.

And so I eat…

Plus Thirty Pounds…

I have made myself an appointment today at the doctors surgery for after school, even though I really hate seeing the doctor at the best of times. He's so black and white and logical and not easy to talk to at all, but I need some help now, REAL help. This craving for food is terrifying me and I just can't seem to stop doing it at all. The weight is piling back on and I am sinking lower and lower into despair. There has to be something he can give me to curb my appetite somehow. What about these diet pills I've heard of? With any luck I can persuade him to give me some of those, just till I can get my own willpower back again.

I hang onto this thread of hope all through the day at school and I count down the minutes to my appointment at half past four. I feel I have no other way out of this nightmare. He simply HAS to help. After all, he is a professional—he must know what to do. He'll have at least SOME answers, won't he?

******

But I guess I should know better by now really, shouldn't I? After all the disappointments I have been through, all the times I have been let down by the adults in my life who barely even notice I exist, why should I have hoped that another one of them would listen to me at all?

Oh, Dr. Mackenzie listens to what I have to say, but so half-heartedly and he doodles on his notepad all the while I am speaking as if he has far better things to do than listen to me spilling my heart out to him. I tell him that my eating patterns are wildly out of control, that I can't stop myself wanting to eat sweet foods, and that I am putting on weight at a tremendous rate. I tell him I need help. I really need some help to put a stop to all this. Please? Can you help?

"How much do you weigh at the moment?" he asks me when I have paused for breath. I tell him. I know exactly as I weighed myself this morning and was disgusted at what the scales told me. I have put on thirty pounds since that day back in August when I ate those damned liquorice sweets. Thirty pounds?? I am so ashamed of myself and I look down at my feet as I tell Dr Mackenzie what I weigh now.

"Well, there's nothing wrong with that at all" he tells me. "In fact you could actually do to put a little bit of weight ON never mind be worrying about taking it off. The more you eat right now the better! "

"But I can't STOP eating!" I cry desperately. "It's driving me crazy!"

He isn't even taking me seriously now. He has a small smile forming on the corners of his lips and I feel so incredibly patronised. Can't he see how bad this is for me? Isn't he supposed to be here to help?

"You shouldn't even be thinking about trying to stop eating." is his totally insensitive answer. "I see from your notes that you were in hospital fairly recently after collapsing due to under eating. You young girls today seem to be obsessed with losing weight and it really is quiet dangerous, you know. Have you any idea the effect that starving can have on a growing body…"

But his words are drowned out by a loud screaming inside my head as the fear and the panic reach a desperate crescendo inside my skull. There isn't one single thing he can tell me about starving or losing weight or diets or bingeing that I don't already know. I could write a book about it all. I have more knowledge of eating disorders in my little finger than he will ever have. I know all about what it is like—now what I need is the help to dig me out of it, but what is the point?

…"So for heavens sake get this notion of needing to eat less right out of your head, okay?"

Is he finished now? It seems so. I nod to him, defeated and totally dejected, and I walk out of the surgery with my head hung low and fighting the urge to scream and cry and kick out at the world. I walk straight into the supermarket next door to the health centre, where I make my way to the shelves of chocolate bars and pick up a packet of three Twix's. What does it matter now if I eat or not? I wanted help, I needed help, and it took me such a lot of courage to actually swallow my pride and ask for help and what did I get but a stupid lecture on 'young girls today'. Yes, what is the point?

No one is going to help me, it seems and I certainly can't help myself right now. I am trapped in this spiral of self-destruction and I can see no way out of it at all. There is nothing else for me to do but eat my way through this terror once again and head towards a welcome sugary stupor.

And so I eat...

Plus Forty Pounds...

How my life has changed in such a short period of time. I simply can't recognise myself now, either physically or emotionally. My life is a complete mess with no foundation, nothing secure to hold onto, and I stumble from day to day in a sugar-laden haze. I make constant promises to myself that I will break this terrifying chain of self-destruction but I break every single promise almost as soon as I have made it. I take almost a perverse pride in proving to myself just what a hopeless, pathetic case I am.

However, not everything in my life is quite the same. I now have a new 'partner-in-crime', a bingeing partner, and so my splurges of overeating are not always solitary, as they were when they first began.

Sue is in my year at school and she has an eating problem too, just like me. She used to be a really great gymnast and was entered into junior competitions all over the UK—really successful she was too. But then she was injured in a very bad fall and now she can't do gymnastics at all and her promising career is over before it really began. She had to stay off school for such a long time after her fall and that is when the excess food became *her* companion as well and she just can't stop eating at all. Thank God it isn't just me...I never thought I would find anyone like me.

She binges too—great big binges just like me. We can tell each other what we eat and know that we won't be judged at all. I never ever thought I would be able to admit to another human being what I did behind closed doors, especially after telling the doctor and getting nothing but ridicule from him, but with Sue it is different. I think we both sense the desperate need in each other to share what we do and it is tremendously easy to say to her, "Yes, I do that, too." And so now we share our guilty secret, and once or twice a week we even share our bingeing sessions, which is amazing for me. No one has ever seen me binge before.

In some ways it is an almighty relief to know Sue, as she is the only person on this earth who really understands what it is like to be driven by this incredibly strong craving for food. But then there is a down side to it as well, as we just egg each other on all the time. I can be having a relatively good day and then meet up with Sue who has her schoolbag filled with food for a binge, and I am lost yet again. And vice versa, as well, of course. It is a lot easier to keep on bingeing and not have to try to stop if there is someone else who is also doing it alongside you. Not that I think for a moment that I COULD stop anyway. It is my way of life now, horrendous though it is.

Life has fallen into a familiar pattern these days. I buy food on the way home from school and I eat some of it whilst locked away in the bathroom when I get in. It is the only place I can be sure I won't be disturbed and even then I have to stay alert in case someone comes up the stairs and discovers me somehow. I don't know how, but I have such a guilty conscience these days that I am constantly on red alert.

Then I have my tea as normal so as not to arouse suspicion—Nanna is SO relieved that I am eating proper meals again and I hate the fact that she is so happy to see me piling on all this weight. I resent her pleasure in my downfall and my increasing body size and we have many fights these days as I feel she is so against me and all that I want for myself. But that's a whole other story…

After tea I either go up to my room and devour what is left of the food I bought earlier or I wait for Sue's phone call to say that her parents have gone out and it is safe to go round to her house with the rest of my booty. By the time I get there, which only takes about ten minutes, Sue has the chip pan going. She is far more into savoury food for her binges than me and we hardly ever share the food we each have, as our needs are so different. We both know how important it is to eat just the right food at this time and so we eat our respective foods alongside each other.

I could never overeat in front of anyone else but it feels so different with Sue because she is doing just the same as I am. The shame of what I do is lessened somehow and I feel more like a naughty schoolgirl than someone in the midst of a terrible addiction. There is even an element of fun to it all sometimes and we can have a laugh about what we eat, even though we both hate the way we live our lives. We even wash down our food with a mouthful or two of her dad's whiskey some nights and then water it down so that he won't see that some has gone missing. Surely one day he will figure it out but right there and then we just don't care what we do.

After it is all over we have to go for a walk to dispose of all the food wrappers in bins far away from her house. We make sure we spray the house with masses of air freshener too, to get rid of the smell of frying chips and by the time her mum and dad come back home we are watching TV as if we have done nothing else all night.

"Good night, girls?"

"Great, thanks."

Great...we have consumed about ten thousand calories each and we feel utterly sick, plus we have taken laxatives as well and we're just waiting for them to absorb into our systems and do their worst...

Oh, yes...it is with Sue that I discover the 'joy' of laxatives. Her mum has a bottle of Syrup of Figs in the house and one night we share the whole bottle between us in the vain hope that it will somehow get rid of all the food we have eaten that night. It tastes awful and I am nearly sick just drinking it, but I make myself do it as it feels as if I may just have discovered an answer to these nightly binges. I have no other option now, not that I know of anyway. If I can't stop myself putting the food INTO my mouth and I can't make myself sick (I've still had no luck there, but it's not for the want of trying) then I have to find some other way to get the food out.

The first time I take them I wake up in the middle of the night with horrendous stomach cramps and I barely make it to the bathroom in time. I sit doubled over in agony as waves of nausea wash over me and I am soon bathed in sweat and shaking from head to toe. By the time I return to my bed for the seventh time that night, for this purging is very persistent, I feel as if I am totally empty. My stomach is still cramped and very painful, I am nearly at the point of fainting with the pain, but I feel empty and that is all that matters to me right now. Climbing back weakly into bed I feel a strange sense of satisfaction creep over me. I haven't felt this way in a long long time...at last I think I have found a way out of this nightmare...I have an escape route...

******

Before too long taking the laxatives has become a daily occurrence. I go to school each day in such pain and discomfort and sometimes I need to rush to the toilets at school which is so very embarrassing but even that doesn't put me off taking the laxatives or having the binges in the first place. I don't think anything could stop me now. If someone came up to me and announced that if I had one more chocolate bar or drank one more mouthful of Syrup of Figs after a binge I would die, I still wouldn't be able to stop. I am so enmeshed in this way of life, and it is all I can think about from the moment I wake until the moment I fall into a gluttonous lethargy last thing every night.

I tell myself after every bottle (for it's a full bottle of laxative mixture that I take now) that THIS time will be my last. I will get rid of this food inside me and then I will NEVER do it again. I won't binge tomorrow, I won't take the laxatives, and I will start to really live again instead of stumbling from day to day in this awful haze. But who am I kidding? I know even as I say those words to myself that it would take an absolute miracle to stop me now and it has just become part of the habit to say that tomorrow will be different. I so want it to be different, but God knows how it ever will be. Every day just becomes the same pain-ridden, guilt-laden mountain of sugar as the one before.

And then one terrible day, Nanna finds a half-drunk bottle of Syrup of Figs in my schoolbag. I am so very angry that she has been looking in my bag anyway, and I don't really care if she is just worried about me as she claims she is. She has no right to go sneaking through my things like that. My immense shame and guilt that she now suspects me of taking the laxatives makes me even more angry and I scream at her in utter despair.

"It's not even mine! It's Sue's!" (Oh, what a very loyal friend I am…)

"Then I'd better get on the phone to Sue's mum and tell her just what's going on." Nanna persists which is even worse so I confess and tell her that it IS my bottle but that it was a one off thing and I promise that it'll never ever happen again.

"It better not," she warns me, and she throws the rest of the syrup down the sink in the kitchen. I watch her in horror and feel just as I imagine an alcoholic would feel if his last bottle of whiskey were emptied out before his eyes. That was my lifeline for tonight. I needed it to get rid of the excess food that is still lodged in my stomach, and now the shops are closed and there is no way I can get any more at all.

I hate Nanna for what she has done to me tonight and vow that I'll carry on living the way *I* want to live despite what SHE wants. SHE can't control me, nobody can. She can't take this away from me. NEVER.

I wait until she has gone upstairs then I get quickly on the phone to Sue.

"Sue, it's Anne. This is an emergency. I don't suppose you have any spare laxatives, do you? I'm desperate."

Plus Fifty Pounds…

How Can I Do This?

How can I do this?
Over and over again without fail?
Always vague promises –
No more, no more.
Always begging, please, no more…

Yet each day it is just the same.
Tomorrow is another day.
A fresh start which never comes.
And all the time I hate myself even more
For slowly dragging
A blade through my heart.

******

There is a boy in my class at school called Mike. We are doing French and German 'A' level classes together and so we see each other quite a lot through the week and for some reason he has decided he likes me. I am bewildered by this as no other boy at school even notices me, especially now I have put so much weight back on. But I am also over the moon by the sudden attention that Mike gives me and my heart leaps when he talks to me or even looks at me. He isn't even one of the geeks either! He's okay looking and he is quite accepted by the other kids in the class—and he likes ME!!!!! This is unbelievable!!

Of course he has no idea at all about the extent of my food problems and I have no intention of ever telling him or else he would surely run a mile in the opposite direction. So I always act perfectly normally around food when he's there. Plus, having him as part of my life gives me an added incentive to lose weight again, doesn't it? Nobody wants a fat girlfriend, do they? Wow, do you think someone could actually want ME for a girlfriend?? I can't stop thinking about it and wondering if this is for real??

I am so very self-conscious about my body though and I spend absolutely ages every time I am going out with Mike, even if it's only to his house, trying to decide which clothes to wear out of my ever-decreasing wardrobe. Which clothes can I find that will adequately cover up the rolls of fat which seem to grow bigger every day. I am so ashamed of how I look and spend so long trying in vain to disguise the fact that I am getting fatter and fatter as time goes by.

I needn't bother really, as Mike doesn't pay me much attention physically, if you know what I mean. Oh, we hold hands when we go out together now and he always gives me a peck on the cheek when he walks me home at the end of the night, but I can understand why he doesn't kiss me properly or even do more. It's because of the way I look; it simply has to be. If I could only lose some weight again then he would treat me like a *proper* girlfriend, so I know it all boils down to me and I'm just so grateful that he pays me any attention at all, because no one else at school does. Now that I am putting on the weight again, I have gone back to being Emma's 'Nonentity' in most people's eyes and none more so than in my own…

******

Tonight I am sitting by the telephone, watching the seconds slowly tick by on the clock on the wall beside me. Mike and I are supposed to be going out tonight and he said he'd ring me at seven to let me know when and where to meet. But it's twenty past seven already and the phone hasn't rung once tonight.

I've been so good today as well and I have hardly eaten anything, just so that I could squeeze into my black jeans a little easier. I've only had one bowl of low calorie soup and an apple, but it's worth it for Mike. I've done my makeup all nice—despite Nanna's loud protests that I've got too much 'muck' on my face. She hates me wearing makeup especially now there is a male involved in my life. I'm sure she thinks I am going to end up like my Mum or my Aunty, who both had disastrous relationships with men, and she is so suspicious of my blossoming friendship with Mike. I'm sure she doesn't believe me when I tell her we haven't even kissed properly yet. She most certainly doesn't have to worry about ME coming home and announcing I am pregnant! The way things are going with Mike, it would have to involve a whole lot of divine intervention for that to happen!

And still I sit and wait for him to call. Why is he always late like this? I've lost count of the times he said he would phone and didn't, or he has arranged to see me and then forgotten to turn up. I always forgive him though. No matter how upset I am, I forgive him because I am afraid that if I make him angry with me he will just want to stop seeing me and right now he is the only good thing I have going for me in my life. I can't lose him whatever he does to me…

It's half past eight now and at last I have to admit to myself that he's forgotten me again. Nanna says I am a mug for putting up with the way he treats me and deep down I know what she says is true, but what else can I do? She just doesn't understand at all how much I need him. He makes me feel almost normal somehow. Somebody wants to be with me, and that counts for a lot.

Maybe I should call HIM instead? There's still time to go out if I call him now. But I don't want to put him under any pressure or have him think that I am chasing him. What if he thinks I am pestering him? God, this is so hard…why didn't he just call me like he said he would?

I dial his number. His mum answers on the third ring.

"Sorry, love, he's gone put with Martin and the gang. They've gone to some night-club in the town for a birthday party. Can't remember exactly where now…"

But it doesn't matter, as I know just where he has gone. He has gone to the party that WE were supposed to be going to together. How could he have forgotten that he asked me to go with him? Why did he forget me? What is it about ME? Don't I mean anything to him? I put down the phone, almost in tears and go upstairs quickly before Nanna can say I told you so.

And so I eat…

What's the point of starving myself now anyway? There's no party for me to go to, no one to impress, no one but me, and I hate myself so much right now that I don't blame him for preferring to be out with the gang than with me. A fat cow like me hanging on his arm would be the last thing he needed.

I change out of the black jeans I have poured myself into, and curl up on my bed in my baggy old nightie, tucking into a huge bowl of cornflakes, laden with sugar. Then I go downstairs for another one, despite the looks Nanna gives me, and I eat and eat until the painful emptiness I feel inside has been pushed far enough down not to matter any more, for today at least.

Plus Sixty Pounds…

It is a less than a month away from Christmas and I have decided that this year, to save a little money, I will make everybody homemade selection boxes as gifts. That way I can buy people all the kinds of chocolate they like best and it'll be a whole lot more fun. Besides, if I am buying the chocolate for someone else and not for me, then no way will I eat it, will I? I'd feel far too guilty to do that.

I've been really good these past three days actually. For the first time in longer than I care to remember I have stuck to my diet and have only eaten what I have written down on my chart. I have only had 650 calories each day and I've gone back to my exercise routine again as well, so at least I have managed to find a little more of my old control and that makes me feel so hopeful for the future. Okay, so I know that I have more than sixty pounds to lose now, but I did it before and I am certain I have the willpower to do it again if I put my mind to it. Wouldn't it be amazing if I could lose a whole chunk of weight before Christmas and my birthday? What a fantastic gift that would be to myself, not to mention Mike! I feel so very strong right now, as if there is nothing that could shake me off this path again. I feel invincible!!

******

I have bought ten chocolate bars today as a start to the selection boxes. I cover them in lovely gold Christmas paper as soon as I get in from the shops so that I can't even see their wrappers and I place them in a big tin underneath my bed. They are safe and out of the way of temptation there. I feel really proud of myself for my willpower and I feel such a surge of that old strength coming back to me. I can do it all again, can't I? I CAN…

******

It is ten o'clock that same night and I carefully unpick the sellotape on the wrapped up bars of chocolate, as even in this manic state of mind I am conscious that I can maybe use this paper again and all will not be lost. I came to bed ten minutes ago, totally unprepared for the sudden craving I would have to eat all that chocolate hidden under the bed. I have done so well today as well. I have had 602 calories in all and I did double rations of exercise after my tea which made me feel so very good about myself. I didn't even feel the remotest pangs of hunger when I came up to bed.

Then it was just as if my whole mind, my whole being was engulfed with the image of that tin of chocolate underneath the bed. All my senses were bombarded with it. I could see it as an enormous living picture in my mind;

I could almost hear it calling to me. I could taste the sweetness on my tongue already, smell the gorgeous creamy richness of the chocolate and feel the smoothness of it as it slipped down my throat. It was as if I was watching it on a giant TV screen in front of me and I wanted to dive right in there and be part of the picture too. I tried to push the image out of my mind as much as I could, but I could no more do that than move a mountain at that moment in time. So, like a zombie, like someone being controlled by another being, I reached down under my bed and pulled out the tin.

All the wrapping paper is off now and I have this one last chance to turn back and resist the temptation, but I can't. I just can't. It has gone far beyond temptation and now it's a case of HAVING to eat the chocolate or…or what? I'm not even sure what will happen but I know that if I force my mind to think along those lines then I am absolutely engulfed in a terror that overwhelms me and sends me running straight back to my safety net of food.

I eat all the chocolate bars one by one, not even tasting the last two or three as my taste buds have become numbed to the sweetness and I just eat them because there is no other option now. To leave them behind would be setting up a disaster for tomorrow before it had even begun. There is no enjoyment in what I am doing, not after the first couple of bars anyway. I eat them because I HAVE to…it is as simple as that.

I feel so very sick now, so very guilty and so disgusted with myself yet again. All that chocolate has gone in what…twelve minutes? All that money was just wasted. The money in my Post office savings account is really starting to dwindle now and I daren't ask Nanna for any more pocket money. She would go mad if she knew just how much I was drawing out of my account every week and spending on food. But whatever, I'll have to replace them all again and start my selection boxes from scratch. Next time I must put them somewhere I can't reach them so easily through the night.

******

I hide the next ten bars of chocolate that I buy in a box behind the settee downstairs, telling Nanna not to look in it as it contains Christmas presents. I hate going downstairs in the dark at night as I still have this childlike fear of the dark and I hate this house at night. The blackness is all encompassing and it has this almost physical presence which chills me to the bone. Surely that will put me off looking for the chocolate through the night?

But of course it doesn't. I've eaten twenty bars altogether now…

******

I hide the next ten bars in Nanna's room, because I hardly ever go in there, but then I wait until I can hear her snoring through the wall and then I creep in to get them. Thirty bars now...

With the next ten bars I give up all pretence that they will ever make it into a homemade selection box. Oh, I am still telling myself out loud that that's the reason I am buying them, but I know deep down that they will end up being mine. I don't even bother to wrap them up this time as what is the point in wasting that effort when I know I will just be ripping the paper off later that same day? I just leave them in the tin under my bed now, waiting for bedtime and darkness to fall. Forty bars...

And so the trend continues and by December 20 I have given up completely on the idea of homemade selection boxes, as they will never happen. I have also given up on being able to last more than three days in a row on a diet, as I haven't been able to manage one single good day since I started buying the chocolate. I have eaten one hundred and sixty bars of chocolate in sixteen days...how the hell could I have done that? It is gross, it is obscene, it is foul, revolting, and disgusting...I am all of those things and much much more. I am a total waste of space, I am greedy, weak, and obnoxious, I don't deserve to live. What would people think of me if they only knew what I did behind closed doors? They would hate me as much as I hate myself if that were at all possible.

And so I eat some more. I am a totally lost cause. What does it matter now if I eat or not?

Plus Seventy Pounds...

Today I am making myself confront yet another evil that I have brought back into my life over the past few months and over the past seventy pounds in weight that has attached itself to me. It is something that I so desperately want to pretend isn't happening or else I want to believe so badly that it is someone other than me who is doing all of this. But I can't. Not anymore.

I can barely write down the words I need to use, but I know I have to make myself do it. I can no longer cope with keeping yet another guilty secret completely inside myself and I have to get it out somehow. It is driving me crazy. I can't tell anyone else, but I simply must make the big step of at least admitting it to myself in black and white.

I steel myself…come on, do it! Don't chicken out now!

Okay, here goes…

A few of those chocolate bars that I got, supposedly for the selection boxes, and plenty of other things besides them…all of that food…well…

God, this is so hard to admit even to myself and much harder to actually put down in black and white.

Okay, take another deep breath….a lot of the food that I have eaten recently has been stolen. By ME. There…I have said it. I feel shaky and sick but at least it is out.

Yes, I am a thief. A shoplifter. I steal.

I either steal the food I want from whatever shop I can, or else I steal the money with which to buy the food. I use precious little of my savings account or my pocket money to buy any of the excess food I smuggle daily into the house. Not anymore anyway. In fact, I hate to have to give my own money away in order to buy this disgusting food. Not that my pocket money and the meagre amount that I earn from my few hours at the newsagent's would even begin to cover what I spend on food each week anyway, but I still don't want to spend *that* money if I could possibly help it. My addiction is bad, it is tainted, and it is shameful…I simply can't spend my own money on *that*.

I take such awful risks to get what I want these days, what I NEED…but at the time I just don't care if I get caught and the dreadful consequences of my actions are almost blanked out in my mind, as if they wouldn't really happen to me anyway. Besides, it has been so incredibly easy up to now, even though I know this sounds so arrogant. I know so very well that it is wrong and that it goes against everything I have been brought up to believe, but I cannot stop. I still vividly remember the absolute shame that I felt when Nanna found out I had taken those stupid stickers all those years ago, but even that doesn't put me off at all. I just can't see right from wrong anymore when it comes to the food. I need it—I take it. It's that simple.

It's especially difficult to keep my hands off the chocolate when I am working at the newsagent's on a Sunday. My boss, Barry, leaves me on my own for most of my four hour shift and sometimes he goes out altogether and I'm completely at liberty to choose whatever I want from the shelves and put it into my bag without anyone there to see what I am doing. I've also started taking a few pounds here and there out of the till which never gets noticed as Barry's till is one of those old fashioned ones which doesn't even have a proper till roll and it is so very easy just to 'forget' to ring up the occasional purchase. Then I just take the money out again later on when I am by myself and no one is ever any the wiser. I am so lacking in morals right now that I even spend some of this stolen money in the shop itself when Barry comes back and takes over from me at the end of my shift. He never knows, he never even suspects.

It's as if there are two people in my body right now—the upright and honest citizen, hardworking, generous, always ready to help anyone and be all I can be to people. Then there is this 'other' side of me which would do anything at all to get my daily 'fix', and which doesn't even acknowledge the deceitfulness and dishonesty of my actions. I just cannot allow myself to think of this in a calm, rational way because it is far too terrifying and I hate to think of what I am becoming and what I am being driven to because of my need for food. I don't know quite what I am capable of anymore and that is so very frightening. There is no black and white in my life today…I am swimming in this giant vat of grey soup and each day I get a little closer to drowning completely.

And so I eat, again and again, especially when the guilty feelings rear their ugly heads and I am hit by the enormity of what I am doing just to have enough food for my soul. It's never for my body, always my soul. Not that there can EVER be enough for me really. I always turn to my food, whatever is happening in my life. It is my magical drug and it makes the outside world disappear and turns the awful grey soup into a comforting blanket of chocolate and biscuits and cake and in that very moment, nothing else in the world matters to me any more…

Plus Eighty Pounds…

Why The Torture?

Why the torture? Why the pain?
Why these senseless thoughts again?
Why the anguish? Why the doubt?
I just can't get these feelings out.

They twist inside—it hurts so much,
Can't even smile, don't want to touch,

Can't understand what's going on,
I wonder where my strength has gone.

I know that this just has to be,
To get it out, to get to me.
But times like this I wonder when
This craziness is going to end...

******

My schoolwork used to be so very simple for me—most of the time anyway. I've always been clever, bright and quick and I'm so used to being able to carry out whatever work I have to do without too much bother. But now...now it's almost as if my brain has ceased to function properly and I stare down at my homework, willing it to make some sense. I read over the same lines again and again, and I still can't understand what I'm supposed to do.

Classes in school are even worse as I am humiliating myself on a daily basis in front of people who seem to take pleasure in my downfall. I see them snigger behind my back, I hear the comments about how big I have got, how I'm not as clever as I used to be, and don't I just know it? It feels just like it used to before I lost all the weight in the first place. I am reduced to being a big fat Nothing again, except now I am stupid as well as a great big Loser.

The pressure on me from Nanna and my teachers is enormous. I am expected to 'fulfil my potential' and as my marks slip I cannot fail to see the disappointment in their faces and my already battered self-esteem slips down another few notches. I would never have thought it was possible to sink so low. I keep thinking that THIS has to be it and I can't sink any lower than I already have. THIS is the day I will curl up and die, when I will slip away in my sleep after treating my body so badly, and I am always surprised and more than a little disappointed when I wake up in the morning to face yet another ordeal of a day.

My form tutor keeps speaking about the future—about me going to College or University, about what course I want to apply for, what do I want to do with my life? I sit there silently and cannot even find the words to begin to explain to him how I feel about my future. I have no interest at all in going to University. The last thing I want to think about is a career. I can't even face the thought of being an adult and going out into this big wide world without a dozen bars of chocolate in my hand, and even then I can't imagine it for too long. I can't see past this everlasting food nightmare at all. Nothing else exists except around the fringes of the food and even then it is so blurry and unreal. School is unreal, home is unreal and my future and my whole life is unreal. I don't even know if I HAVE a future. How much longer can my body face this incessant pummelling?—the almost daily binges, the daily handfuls of laxative drinks and pills, the occasional bouts of absolute starvation when I actually seem to get some element of control back into my life. Then there are the futile attempts I have made at regaining some kind of sanity—the acupuncture, the hypnotherapy sessions. Nothing at all has worked for me. Nothing can break through this desperate need I have for the food, or the equally desperate yearning I have to stop.

I live with voices in my head every day. Voices that tell me to eat, voices that argue with the first lot of voices and beg me not to, voices of reason, voices of insanity, voices of the old me and voices of this crazy being I have become. Amidst these voices I am supposed to concentrate on teachers talking about European History, I am meant to learn reams of German vocabulary, I am meant to write essays on French literature. My whole life feels as if it is hanging on a very thin thread and I have to listen to lectures about wearing the right school uniform. My mind is falling apart and I am told off constantly for daydreaming. I wish…

And so I eat…I eat and eat and I don't think I will ever be able to stop now. I will eat myself to death, I know it. I will die with a bar of chocolate in my hand. I will keep on killing myself slowly but surely because right now I can't seem to get off this manic merry-go-round.

My French essay still sits undone in front of me; just the title is written down at the top of the page, and I can't for the life of me even remember what those few words mean. In the end I push it aside and crawl into my bed, so very very tired. Too tired to think, to remember, to concentrate, to formulate, but never ever too tired to eat. I slowly and automatically break off a chunk of chocolate from the constant supply beneath my bed and I fall asleep as it melts gently in my mouth…

Plus Ninety Pounds…

Self-Destruction

So many times I destroy myself needlessly
With thoughts and doubts which should never be.
I destroy my pride, my self-respect, and my confidence
Until there is nothing left but a gaping hole
Where a person used to be.

I know so well that my misery is self-made,
Yet I cannot control the gradual decay of my dying soul.
My mind plays evil tricks on me.
It eats away slowly at the certainty
Leaving only a huge mountain of doubt
Which haunts me day and night,
Increasing in strength minute by minute
Until it reaches the crazy heights of paranoia
And finally crushes me completely.

******

Empty spaces, always empty spaces.

Inside me, in my head, in my heart, in my soul.

I am never complete.

Never a whole person.

Never real.

Never valuable.

Never deserving of my place here on earth.

I am no one.

Nothing.

A nonentity.

Without the food I am nothing.

Without the anorexia I am nothing.

With the food I feel full if only for a little while.

With the anorexia I had control over my life, I had a structure, a framework.

Now I have nothing.

I AM nothing.

I only ever exist as something to somebody else; Nanna's granddaughter, Gayle and Diane's sister, Mike's friend.

Other people give me a shape and a reason for being there, but when I am alone I disappear and my whole being sinks into a deep bottomless pool and I am lost.

The bold outlines that other people have drawn around me to give me substance disappear and I cannot hold myself together alone.

I crumble.

I spill over the edges.

I cease to exist.

I am engulfed by this fear and panic, and only food can make it go away.

And so I eat…

And the food fills the void and for a moment I feel as if someone has drawn the black lines around me again and I am a real person.

Just for a moment until the food becomes too much and takes over my whole being.

The food gives me substance and blocks out the terror.

Except, once I start eating I cannot stop and the bold blacks lines around me stretch and stretch even more and threaten to burst and destroy me completely.

I still cannot stop.

I have to eat and eat until every last corner of my being is saturated with food and there are no empty spaces left inside of me.

At all…

Chapter Four
Chocolate Versus Life

Setting the Scene...

I can't believe it has been three whole years since that momentous day back in February 1978 when I turned my whole world upside down. Three years since the day I decided that *this* time I would show everyone just how strong I really was. Three years since the day I vowed that *this* diet was going to be the one that changed my life. And boy, did it ever change my life. I have never been the same since and my existence has altered beyond all recognition.

Whether that is a good thing or not, I can't quite figure out yet, as I am still swimming around here in my grey soup, but there have been glimmers of light here and there, and I actually have days where I have a little hope. Just a tiny glimmer of hope here and there, but it's bit of an improvement on the total blackness I had before, isn't it?

My life is so very predictable now and I have fallen into a way of living that isn't much more than a bare existence really. But at least it is a little more bearable than some of the days I have lived through in the past and that has to be good, doesn't it? I am an adult now, or at least I am attempting to live an adult life, and I am far from being at peace with that, but I live it the best way I know how until I can hopefully find a better way to be.

It feels as if I have two very distinct personalities inside my head during this period of my life, with each 'person' battling against the other on a daily basis for prominence and victory. There is the 'Good' side of me which always tries to cut back on my food, attempts to do as much exercise as possible, tries to lose weight, gain confidence and simply be a better ME. And then there is my 'Bad' side which attempts to do just the opposite and succeeds on far too many occasions.

It is as if I have incorporated both the anorexic and bulimic sides of me into my very soul and they live unhappily alongside each other every day. I swing between the two of them on a regular basis and there is absolutely nothing in-between. One day I will live by the rules of the 'Good' side of me, but the very next day I can be firmly on the side of the 'Bad'. Most days I wake up being one of them and then I can turn into the other in an instant throughout the day for no apparent reason—it's usually Good to Bad though, not the other way around. It is a complete living nightmare when the Bad takes over. I wake up each morning and am never quite sure just who I am going to be that day. Which voice will speak up the loudest today? Who am I this morning?

I still have so many binges but they have lessened in ferocity a little, and they don't happen every single day like they used to be. But the feelings I have along with them, the intense cravings I have to reach out for food stay the same and my head is never really at peace. Even whilst I sleep I have dreams where I am working my way through a mountain of food and I wake up terrified that it is actually true. The relief I have when I find out it was just a bad dream is incredible. The only real break I get from the cravings is when I manage a few days of eating precious little and then I get that wonderful heady rush that comes with this voluntary starvation. But that doesn't happen very often, and certainly not often enough to have any real impact on my steadily rising weight.

Over the past three years I have lost one hundred and twenty pounds in weight, many times over, I'd imagine, but then I have managed to put it all back ON and much much more besides . I am one hundred and eighty pounds heavier than the day I ate those liquorice sweets—isn't that awful? It disgusts me, it really does, but I feel no more able to do anything to rectify it than I did three years ago. Pathetic, isn't it? I am an adult now and I still have so little power over my life.

Today I would say that I am a Compulsive Eater, as that is mainly what I do. The laxative abuse still happens, but not as regularly as before, so I'm not really bulimic any more, but neither am I anywhere near approaching normal when it comes to food. I often wonder if I ever will be. Can you ever be normal again after going through all this? I can never imagine myself just getting up and having a normal breakfast and then not thinking about food again until lunchtime…That would be just incredible…

The rest of my life is a *little* more settled than it was back then…

Let me catch you up on a few things…

There are just Nanna and I living at home today and life is much more peaceful here than before. Aunty has married now and the whole family live two houses away from us, so we see them all just about every day. Nanna is a lot more relaxed now that she has her home back, and that makes a tremendous difference to the way we get on. Plus, I am eating regularly (*very*!) and so she has one less worry on her mind. She still has no idea about my binges—at least I *hope* she doesn't—but I have gained weight in front of her eyes over the years so she must realise I am eating more than she sees. She says nothing though—she probably daren't rock the boat and I can't say I blame her. No way would she want me to lose weight again, yet that is still my greatest desire and I work at it every single day.

At last I have some peace and privacy in my own home which means the world to me. I can retreat to my bedroom every night after tea and know that I won't be interrupted by anyone. I switch on my stereo, put on my headphones and listen to loud music and just let myself be taken wherever I want to go. Music has become a real passion in my life, and I have actually found something that frees my mind from its obsession with food, if only for a short time. I *live* the music, I AM the music, I can lose myself in it and feel every emotion possible whilst the notes flood through me. It is truly a lifesaver and remains so to this day.

And yes…most nights I also eat the food that I have bought through the day and smuggled upstairs when Nanna wasn't looking. I eat, I sing, I dance, and then I go back downstairs and watch the TV. This is my new way of life.

Some nights I go out with Mike, who is still very much a part of my life. Sadly, we remain nothing more than 'just good friends' although everyone else believes that we have a 'proper' relationship going on. If only…We see each other three or four times a week, we go to the pub, we go out for meals, or to parties, but at the end of each night we go home alone and I never stop wondering why. I am too afraid to bring the subject up though just in case it is too much for him and I frighten him away. Also I am afraid that he will say the words that are always buzzing around in my head—'it's because I don't find you attractive, I don't want you'—I am so afraid of hearing that, and so I keep quiet as always. At least I have *someone* in my life, and let's face it, I never thought I would have *anyone*.

I work now too, as a Care Assistant in a residential home for physically handicapped adults. It is something I had never thought of doing at all before and I kind of fell into this job by accident, but I have found something that I love to do, and that is to care. It is just a temporary placement and I don't know what will turn up next but for now, this is as good as it's been. I have managed to escape the pressure that was put upon me to go to University, and I have almost overcome that feeling of being a complete failure in everyone's eyes, including my own. I feel as if I am doing something useful with my life for those few hours a day I am working—and let's face it, it keeps me away from the food as well.

Every morning without fail before I go to work, I get weighed and I watch in a kind of numb despair as the needle points to higher numbers by the week. Surely it has to reach a peak ONE day? I surely can't just keep on gaining like this? But then, if I keep on overeating the way I am, it is only logical that I will keep on gaining, isn't it? Any fool could tell you that. It also makes perfect sense that if I want to lose the weight, all I have to do is STOP overeating in this way, but I can no more do that right now than fly to the moon. I feel so useless and inadequate, but I always manage to put on my brave face and go out to work as if I haven't a care in the world. My talents are wasted; I should really have been an actress, shouldn't I?!

When I allow myself some time to daydream and drift off into the realms of fantasy, I imagine that someday someone will magically appear in my life—someone who will make it all okay for me. A kind of knight in shining armour combined with my fairy godmother. Together we will make a perfect 'me', both in body and soul, and then I will be totally protected from all the hurts that life has to throw at me. I will be safe and secure, and nobody will be able to get to me…if only…

That is my dream, but I know things like that don't happen in real life, not for the likes of me anyway.

No, I have kind of come to terms with the fact that this is my lot in life and I have almost settled for this half existence that is mine. Maybe if I felt more worthy of good things happening to me, then I would stand up and fight for more, but most of me feels that even this is more than I deserve really. I know that sounds so pathetic but it is true. I have settled for a mind which is never at peace, an ever-increasing body, a fear of the world around me and a second rate relationship with a man who keeps me at arms length at all times. Not so great really, is it? But it's still more than I feel I deserve sometimes.

And still I eat…because these days I have absolutely no idea what else I should do…

Everything Revolves Around Food…

Food is truly the epicentre of my whole existence, although I hate to admit it, and every last situation that I encounter gets related in some way back to my food or my weight, however twisted it may seem.

My mind is never at peace and I am bombarded constantly with voices in my head telling me what to do and how to behave. I never usually question these voices at all. I simply eat when they tell me to eat, try not to eat when they want me to starve, try to get rid of the food when they say I should…Anything at all to still them for a little while—but I never really ask why or even think of fighting back at them. It would be so very hard and I find it a whole lot easier just to give in and do as they say. It's far less painful that way.

Today is the first time I can really remember listening to those voices properly and answering them back—asking just what this is all about and WHY I do what I do…

I am really freezing today as it is pouring with rain outside and blowing a gale into the bargain. Here I sit, curled up in the armchair with my knees pulled up to my chest, just wearing jeans and a tee shirt and feeling so very cold. I can see the goose pimples growing on my arms and the tiny hairs standing on end and I watch, almost fascinated, as my body reacts to the chill in the house. The wind is whistling through the gaps in the ancient wooden window frames and it immediately obliterates any heat that may be found in the room from the ineffective coal fire. Nanna shakes her head at me and asks me why on earth I don't get myself a jumper if I am so cold.

NO! A voice inside my head shouts at once, and I automatically tell her that I am fine, even though it is blatantly obvious that I am freezing in my tee shirt. Usually that would be enough; the voice tells me, No, and I immediately obey. I usually accept it without question and carry on, but today I begin to think, why on earth am I doing this? Why am I sitting here stone cold when I could so easily wrap myself in a lovely warm jumper and feel so much more comfortable? What is wrong with me?

Because being cold uses up more calories, doesn't it? is the instant reply. And all of a sudden a whole lot of other strange things that I do start to make sense in my rather illogical head, and they are all related to food and weight. Every last thing that I do is in order to use up calories, to lose weight and to be thin. Wow…I never realised quite how bad it was until now.

Why am I suddenly obsessed with going swimming again when even the smell of the chlorine nauseates me after the time I nearly drowned? I didn't go for two years after that incident as I was so afraid of the same thing happening again but now I make myself go and it isn't because I enjoy it at all. It is because it is good exercise, of course, and it uses up those damned calories again.

Why do I refuse to get the bus into town these days and insist on walking, even in the rain? Because it uses up more calories.

When Nanna announced that we were going on holiday to Germany this year, what was my initial reaction? Great? Can't wait? Excitement? No...I got out the calendar and worked out how long it was before we went away and how much weight I could lose by then. And of course I put myself under so much pressure to lose a ridiculous amount of weight that I ended up bingeing and gaining weight instead and having a miserable time because of it...and making Nanna's holiday a misery as well, for which I still feel incredibly guilty.

I have a pretty good social life right now, thanks in the main to Mike, but each event brings up the same crazy thoughts as the holiday...how much weight can I lose before the next night out, the next party, etc? Sometimes I won't even go out if I feel I have failed hopelessly and I don't look anywhere near half-decent as I think I should.

If Aunty asks me to baby-sit for my cousins, it serves two purposes now. It gets me out of the house so that I know I won't binge that night, yet it also gives me more money to go out and buy more food if I DO binge. (Thankfully the shoplifting is something else which plays a slightly lesser part in my life these days and I grudgingly spend money from my own pocket on the excess food.)

I am perversely pleased if I get a bad toothache or I feel really sick as that means I very likely won't eat as much as I normally do. I hate the rare occasions when I am physically sick but I love them too as it means that I have far less food in my system. When I have an upset stomach I feel the same way. I register the pain and discomfort but I am predominantly relieved that I have managed to get rid of some of the poison in my system. Fancy somebody being happy if they are ill? It is so twisted, and yet these are my truths.

Today, for the first time ever, it has really struck me how very much I must hate myself. Oh, I have always known that I did, but I never realised quite how much. I never think twice about putting myself in danger, hurting myself, letting myself suffer—in fact, there is a smug satisfaction within me when I DO suffer. A kind of 'serves you right' mentality, and I seem to be incapable of looking after myself in any shape or form, either mentally or physically. It amazes me...I am an adult and yet I can take care of myself no better than a small, frightened child.

I still can't go against these voices though and I continue to sit here in my jeans and tee shirt and shiver, but at least I have looked the voices square in the eyes today and seen my reality for what it is. Twisted, illogical, incredibly damaging, and oh, so very sad…

Feeling Sorry For Myself

Feeling sorry for myself,
Looking into darkness and seeing no way out.
Just feeling sorry for myself.

I'm wishing things were different now,
That times would change and I'd come out
So much better than I am today
Instead of feeling sorry for myself.

It's my smile's day off today.
I'm letting everybody know
Just how down I am.
I'm shouting, grumpy, being
Just as nasty as I can.
I'm feeling sorry for myself.

I want everything for ME, you see,
Fit into my jigsaw,
Live the way I want you to.
God, how selfish can I be?

Yet it always seems to be the same at times like this,
When I hate each minute of the day
It simply has to pass.
And when I see just how much I really have
I wonder, how could I ever just
Feel sorry for myself?

Telling the Truth…

It is Mike's nineteenth birthday today and we have just been out for a lovely meal together, just the two of us, to celebrate. I don't actually care how much I have eaten tonight as we have had such a close and lovely time together, and besides, I can always take laxatives and starve myself tomorrow to make up for it. I have tried to be 'Good' all week in an attempt to be lighter for tonight, as I really want this birthday to be special for Mike. But as always, I let myself down and ended up bingeing every night, so I had to go out and buy myself something new to wear so I looked as okay as I could for him.

Still, after a few glasses of wine at the restaurant, it hardly seems to matter what I look like or even what I feel like and I relax more than I have been able to in a long time. To make the night even more perfect, Mike agrees to come in for a coffee when he walks me home and my heart just flies. This is just magic. I hate the nights when he says No and just goes home, leaving me feeling so empty and rejected, but tonight he says Yes!!

I feel an excitement I have never known before, as if tonight is going to be more special than I could even have imagined. Nanna has gone to bed, we have the whole living room to ourselves, soft lights, music…maybe, just maybe…but I won't let myself think that way. Just make the coffee, Anne. Don't hope for anything. Deep breaths now…

We settle down with our drinks and I put on some of our favourite music. We talk about the night we have just shared, about our work, and what it feels like to be one year older, and I even feel okay about eating a couple of biscuits with him watching me. I always limit myself to a fairly normal two biscuits when he is around but at least I have the comfort of knowing that I can eat the rest of the packet when he has left. I always like to have a safety net hidden under my bed.

I am sitting on the floor in front of the fire and he is up on the sofa. His legs are beside me and there is such a sense of intimacy that I have never felt with him before, such a closeness between us and my heart is pounding wildly. I never want this night to end at all…I want to hold onto this feeling for the rest of my life. Even the silences feel right; it is so hard to explain but I couldn't have planned this to be more perfect if I had tried.

Then Mike breaks the silence…

"I need to talk to you about something," he begins. "I have something to tell you."

My stomach turns over in excitement, as I imagine what he is going to say. Does he want to say he loves me? Does he want our relationship to go further? The unspoken words hang in the air between us and I am desperate for him to go on.

Then I turn and look up into his eyes and I am suddenly filled with an overwhelming sense of fear. I don't know what warns me but I know that my dreams and my hopes are about to be shattered. This night has been *too* good, *too* magical, *too* perfect. His next few words are going to destroy it all, I know it. I hold my breath and steel myself for whatever is about to happen…

"I'm gay."

He's gay. He's gay. He's gay.

My world comes crashing down around me and a thick grey mist falls down over my eyes as my mind tries to deal with the enormity of what he has just told me. Gay? What? Why? How? When? But…there are no words coming out of my mouth at all and an intense feeling of hopelessness and despair emotionally swamps me.

"Well, say something then," he urges me.

"I…I kind of guessed already," I tell him, which is an outright lie, but later when I think of it, it all makes sense, doesn't it, so maybe at some level I DID know. But not now, not here and now, not tonight when nothing at all makes sense to me. I don't understand any of it at all. It is ME who has the problem, remember? ME who is so incredibly repulsive that you don't want to come near me. ME who turns you off so much that no way would you even contemplate having sex with me. ME!!

Or is it?

"I've known how I've felt for quite a while now," he continues, "but I just didn't know how to tell you. I wanted to say something when we were away in June, but I didn't want to spoil the holiday."

Oh, thanks, I think. So kind of you. So considerate.

"You weren't ever expecting any more than friendship from me, were you?"

God, how blind can he BE? How totally stupidly blind and insensitive to everything I have ever said to him or shared with him can he really be? Did he honestly think it was just a friendship for me? My God!! But I don't say any of this, as I don't want to upset him. HA! Instead I say:

"No. No, of course not. I always knew we were just friends. Don't worry about that."

I am such a frighteningly good liar and that seems to reassure him and he smiles at me and says he is glad, as he didn't want to hurt me. He always wants us to remain friends.

But, oh, I am so so hurt inside right now. I have played the game of "If I just make myself into the person he wants me to be, then one day he'll love me" for so very long that I know no other way to feel about him, about us, about me. One day we'll be a REAL couple. One day I'll be normal. I have clung desperately to those hopes every time he didn't call, every time he ignored me when we were out in a crowd, every time he even forgot we were meant to be going out. One day it will be okay. And now? What now? It will NEVER be okay now…

"We can just carry on the same, can't we?" he is asking me. "I mean, me being gay doesn't put you off wanting to spend time with me, does it? Do you have any problems with the gay thing?"

"Not at all," I tell him which is partly true. One thing I never have been in my life is prejudiced against any colour, race or sexual persuasion. I have always been too busy reserving all my hatred for myself. His being gay would be no problem to me at all if he was just my friend, but I wanted so much more from him and I can't possibly tell him now. Not after tonight.

"Oh, and I haven't told anyone else and I don't really want to, so could you promise me that you won't tell anyone either? Please?"

I nod silently. Of course I won't tell. I am very good at keeping secrets after all. One more won't matter, will it? I'll process it all as I usually do—with ten thousand calories and a packet of laxative pills. No problem…

We talk for a little while longer, but I have no idea what we are talking about as most of my mind is a million miles away, and he must sense that I am really elsewhere as he leaves soon after midnight. Not even a peck on the cheek for me tonight.

I feel as if I have been suspended up high in time and space, with all sense of reality taken away from me. As if in a pre-programmed state, I go into the kitchen, make myself another drink and take it up to bed, to drink along with the rest of the biscuits under my bed.

There is one small redeeming factor in all this, I suppose, not that it makes me feel any better right now. It was never actually ME who repulsed him as such after all. Only in so much as I am totally the wrong sex. Ironic really, that I could have dieted for the rest of my life and I would *still* have never been right for Mike. If I wasn't so terribly low tonight I would laugh. God, all these times I thought it was ME. Why did I never even think it could be HIM?

******

I spend the next few days closeted in my room as much as I can, alternating between bouts of crying and eating. Nanna looks at me funny and asks what's wrong, but I say, Nothing, and she doesn't ask any more. I couldn't tell her anyway, could I? I can't break a confidence so I have to learn to deal with this on my own. I have to keep quiet.

Four days later I call Mike again and we decide to go out for a ride on his motorbike. We go to a nearby seaside town and have a long walk on the beach in the sunshine. I am absolutely desperate to talk more about what he has told me—I NEED to talk so badly. I have so many unanswered questions, and so much I want to clarify in my mind. But when I try to approach the topic he just tells me that he has said all he wants to say on the subject and that we should just consider the matter closed for now. There is nothing more to tell, he says.

I can't believe he can do this to me. How can he tell me something so earth shatteringly big and then zip it back up again as if it didn't matter to either of us? Doesn't he realise the impact he has had on my life? But then I didn't tell him how I felt, did I, so how can he possibly know? We walk back to the bike in silence and he drops me off at home without saying another word. But my mind just cannot stop buzzing with all the unanswered questions I have.

How does he feel? How does he know he is gay? Where do I fit into his life now? Do we have any future at all? What does he want from me? What can I expect from him? What will I do now? Will he ever answer any of these questions?

I have to face up to a lot about myself as well. Like the fact that I have been clinging to him so desperately, hoping that he would be the one who made it all okay and who would bring normality and stability to my life. I had hoped for so much from him and now I have to face the fact that this relationship was never the way I thought it was. At the very bottom of all the mixed emotions I feel today is this tremendous fear that I am going to end up alone. That I am going to be left totally on my own.

I can't face that at all.

I simply cannot be alone.

I cannot just live with ME.

To Be Full…

To be full…what is it like to be full…more than full…bloated, overflowing with food. Just what is it really like?

Tonight I am so full that I feel as if I am going to explode. I have eaten and eaten to dull the pain of the day, or at least to try and turn the emotional pain into a physical pain because that is so much easier to deal with. But the awful sensation of immense physical fullness is never the feeling I am actually looking for when I set out on a binge. I am searching instead for a total release from the pain that is swirling around inside my mind, but in the end I just invite even more fear and discomfort into my day.

My stomach feels so utterly stretched right now and my breathing is far more laborious than usual as my poor lungs are all squashed up inside me. My churning stomach is trying to find yet more room to expand and there is hardly any room left to breathe. I struggle to find each breath and it hurts so much.

There is such a heaviness dragging its way throughout my entire body right now; not just a physical weight but a mental one too, and I am so very tired and sluggish. At this moment in time I don't want even a tiny part of my life any more, certainly not as an adult anyway. If only I could be a child again and sit here crying in a corner until someone came along and rescued me. But it is up to me to rescue myself today, nobody else is going to make it all better, and I'm finding that so incredibly hard to do.

I am physically incapable of much movement at all when I am this bloated. It is so painful to move even a little bit and all I can do is lie down on my bed and wait until some of the food gets digested and makes a little more space in my distended stomach.

Being physically full never makes me want to stop eating though, even when I have gone way past the point of comfort. I can only ever stop when I am *emotionally* full, or should I say emotionally numb. I allow myself to stop when I have finally dulled the pain and can feel nothing at all emotionally. I am feeding my mind or my heart or my soul but hardly ever my body

I feel so very sick just now but I know that I will never actually BE sick, however hard I try. It seems as if my body can consume an inordinate amount of food and never need to part with any of it. I have tried so many ways to make myself sick but nothing works at all and I have given up trying now. Well, almost...I should be grateful really, as that would only give me yet another problem to have to overcome, but despite that, I still wish that I could do it. It would be such an immediate answer to this terrible fullness.

Being full gives me this awful heartburn which washes over me constantly in acidic waves. It lasts for hours after a binge and it will have eased off by the morning only if I am lucky. I can't wait for the time that I feel empty again and I yearn for the hours to pass quickly so that I can be rid of this terrible feeling of bloatedness. It hurts me even to yawn. There is no space...no room at all for me inside my own body.

My poor ravaged heart beats faster and louder as it tries to cope with all the excess work it has to do, and I fear that one day I will have a massive heart attack from all the abuse I constantly throw at my body. I know that I won't get much sleep tonight as my body will be far too hot with all the sugar it has to process. My heart will pound loudly in my ears, my nerves will be tingling, and I will be so uncomfortably hot…

Being full makes me simply want to STOP! Stop living a full life, not that I ever really have, stop working, stop talking, stop socialising, stop facing new challenges, stop BEING completely. Except that I don't actually have the courage to *really* stop myself being and to take my own life. That is one small step too far for me, even though it is so very inviting at times.

…Why do I do this to myself? Over and over again…What comfort do I REALLY find in food? Why do I keep on doing it when I know just what the result will be? When I know just how bad I will feel? It is absolute madness…

Yes, this would seem to be my very own brand of childish tantrum.

My own way of screaming silently at a life which seems so alien to me.

This is how I pout my lip and stamp my feet, just like a stubborn two-year-old who is trying to find her way in the world.

Except nobody seems to notice but me…

Momentary Comfort

It's a momentary comfort, this chosen drug of mine.
It soothes for just a little while,
Placates a stormy mind.
But once the last bite's disappeared
Leaving just a taste behind,
The pleasure turns to guilt and shame
And no peace can I find.

There is no logic to my vice,
No reason that seems clear.
It only aids the here and now—
A momentary cheer.
And in the middle of the night
When pleasure turns to pain
I always take a solemn vow
I won't indulge again.

A vow which lasts for just one day
Then my mind seems to forget
That this comfort lasts for moments
But the pain continues yet...

Pretending to be All Grown-up...

I am sitting in the smoky staff room at work and there are ten minutes left of my break. It is mid morning and I have my usual cup of tea in my hand and a fixed smile upon my face. My eyes dart from one person to another as the conversation makes its way around the room, and I laugh in all the right places and look suitably shocked or saddened when and if it's called for. I am really very good at this!

The dozen or so people I work with are predominantly female, and older than I am and they just seem to ooze with the confidence that I badly lack. They talk to each other with such ease that it amazes me. I feel like a real fraud sitting here alongside all these 'grown-ups' and I stay as quiet as I can for fear of opening my mouth and proving out loud just what an immature kid I really am.

I have a series of temporary jobs after I leave school at the age of eighteen, with my clutch of qualifications in my hand. (I never use a single one of those qualifications, by the way, but my certificates are very impressive!) Some jobs are actually meant to be short-term placements and some I leave myself when I can no longer cope with the demands of this new adult world. My jobs are all in the same field—I either work with physically and mentally handicapped adults or children in some capacity or another. I am a Care Assistant, and then a Nanny to a young girl with cystic fibrosis. I work in a holiday home for disabled people, then as an Occupational Therapy Aide in a hospital and then as a Physiotherapy Aide in a school for physically handicapped children. I never stay in one place for too long, no matter how much I love the work. I find it tremendously difficult to settle anywhere and feel safe.

I can relax so much easier with the children and the adults that I help to look after than with my actual work mates. I feel far more on an equal footing with them, especially the children. I can play with them, laugh with them, understand them, and am able to open up more and just be *me* with them. But the adults I work alongside…well, I still think of them as the REAL grown-ups and beside them I always feel so pathetic and useless. Oh, I try my hardest to fit in, I really do, but I still end up feeling like a pupil who has found her way into the staff room at school by mistake.

I look around me now at the six other women in the room. I am constantly bewildered by the way they can just sit and chat to each other as if it is the easiest thing in the world to do. How can they be that way? Where did they learn this self-confidence? How can they possibly think of all the right things to say so quickly? It baffles me, it really does. The only people I feel anywhere near at ease with in this world are a few family members and my close friends—all two of them, Sue and Mike. With everyone else I have developed a kind of stutter as I generally feel so nervous in conversations and I tend to trip over my words. I try to talk as little as possible to most people so as not to show myself up. Part of me yearns to be right in the midst of these conversations around me, yet the small child within is bewildered by this adult talk and afraid to join in just in case anyone thinks I am stupid. I really wish things were different…

I must admit that I don't exactly make it easy for people to reach out to me and help me to belong, as I am so painfully shy and give very little of myself away. I think even *I* would find it hard to get along with me at this point in time! In my daydreams however, I am right there in the middle of every conversation, throwing my head back with laughter, making everyone else smile, being the life and soul of the party. Ah, that would be great…but in reality I barely utter a word and I blush like a beetroot if anyone so much as looks at me for more than a second.

Every single weekend of my working life I vow to eat as little as possible so that when I go back to work on Monday my clothes will feel slacker. My confidence will therefore be greater and I will actually be able to string two words together and hold an adult conversation. At least that is the theory. But, as always, I put far too much pressure on myself not to eat and I can't seem to find the willpower to exist on 400 calories a day anymore. Monday comes around and I am still the same frightened little girl who hides behind her cocoon of fat. Will it EVER change? I really cannot see how.

And when at last I can no longer take being the self-inflicted "Odd One Out", I make up some excuse about the job not being suitable and I move on. But it is never really the job—it is always ME. I just cannot cope and I can't fit in.

Once again I turn to my food strategies to give me some kind of stability at times like this. When the going gets tough, I write out a food plan. When my life spins out of control, I work out my calories for the day. There is such comfort in these black and white figures and they are always there for me. They never change. I know exactly what to expect from them. Some days they give me immense pleasure when the numbers are low enough and I have been 'Good'. I feel so much safer in my shaky world then. And even if the numbers are too high I can still find some safety there too, as I reach right out for even more food to quash the despair I feel and attempt to numb it all out that way.

Whatever happens in my life, I am okay as long as I have my food, whether it is too much or too little. My food is always there for me when the day has been rough. My food never judges me or laughs at me or makes me feel worthless. My food is just *there* all the time, whenever I need it.

It is my constant lifeline in a very scary adult world…

My Knight in Shining Armour…

Whilst still floundering around in my non-relationship with Mike I meet Neil. It isn't one of those 'our eyes met across a crowded room' moments or anything like that. We actually meet through a computer of all things. I have joined a Computer Dating Agency, as I just can't see any other way of meeting another guy in the small town where I live. Everyone knows me as one half of 'Anne and Mike' and I don't see how it is possible to shake that off. All of our friends have mentally married us off with a couple of kids, but if only they knew what it was really like between us…Of course, they *can't* know as Mike still won't tell anyone else, and so I feel trapped in this 'pretend' relationship. In the end, desperate measures come into play.

Hardly anyone knows I have joined the Agency because I'm pretty ashamed that I need to 'look for a man' this way. I know lots of people do it, but I am convinced that the reasons I am doing it make me into a sad and desperate individual. There is the added fact that Nanna would go berserk if she knew I was spending my money like this. Even though I am in my early twenties now, it still matters a lot that Nanna approves of what I do, so I tend to hide from her the parts of my life that I know she won't like. The fact that I drink occasionally, and yes, I have even been drunk quite a few times in recent years. The fact that I go to nightclubs and parties where there are both women and MEN! My God!! I still put my makeup on where she can't see me as she constantly refers to it as my 'muck' and I feel as if I am a complete slut because I use a bit of eye shadow and mascara. So telling her that I am actively seeking, and paying for, a partner is certainly NOT on the agenda!

Neil is the fourth person I write to and the third person I meet up with. I warm to his gentle manner straight away and I can't believe it when he seems to feel the same way about me. He's a little older than I am (another REAL grown up!), he is a Scotsman and he is serving in the Air force on a tour of Northern Ireland. We see each other once a month when he comes back to England for a week to a flat he shares with some other 'squaddies' and we have a fantastic time together.

First of all I just go to see him for a day, and then the next time is a long weekend and by then I am hooked. We love each other's company, we walk and talk for hours, and yes…we even have a physical relationship!!!!!!!!

My God, I am twenty-two years old and I thought it would never happen for me. Who in their right mind would be attracted to ME, for heaven's sake? Okay, so I am slightly lighter at the moment as I have managed to curb the binges a little over the past year or so and have been a lot more active, but even so, I am still obsessed by food. I always try to avoid it as much as I can, or else I know I will eat ten times as much as any normal person would. I still feel so very guilty every time I eat and I am firmly convinced that I am huge, fat and thoroughly disgusting. I just can't believe that he wants ME…

But when I am with Neil…ah, he makes me feel that maybe, just maybe, I might be wrong about some of the negative things I tell myself. Maybe I'm not quite so bad after all?

He is the first person without an eating problem that I share all my food secrets with. Well, maybe not all of them, but a whole lot more of them than anyone else knows apart from Sue. He doesn't judge me or ridicule me and what's more, he really wants to help and make it all better for me. Could this be the knight in shining armour I have been waiting for? I hardly dare hope…

We go out for meals together and when I feel bloated and guilty afterwards for having so much to eat, we walk and talk until my mind is settled again. He understands that it is so tough for me and he gives me a safe place to talk about how it really IS. For the first time in my life I can find words to explain how I feel, as for the first time someone really wants to listen and understand. I am overwhelmed by the compassion he shows me and I am madly in love with him into the bargain!

He helps me in my attempts to be 'normal' around food and I try to eat proper meals on a daily basis, which is something I haven't done for many years. For the three weeks he is working back in Northern Ireland and I am back home with Nanna, I cook us a real meal every single night. I find I can eat it without bingeing afterwards (mostly) and with just a little less guilt than before. Neil calls me on the phone every night without fail and we talk about our days and he tells me how very proud he is that I am coping so much better with my food. With him in my life I really WANT to do well and to take care of myself now. For the first time ever I have a reason to be good to myself.

A small part of me wakens up during this time, and I begin to have some REAL hope for the future, some hope that my life is maybe going to turn out okay after all. Maybe there will be an end to all this mental torture and I can really be happy.

We marry on April 29th 1985 after knowing each other for just over a year and we move into our first home together at RAF Leuchars, Neil's next posting. Thus begins a whole new journey for me, with more challenges to face as an adult than ever before…

******

Having such a close relationship with a man brings up every single insecurity it was ever possible for me to have! Neil has the patience of a saint as he has to deal with me constantly dissecting our lives together and also his love life before me, and examining it all in minute Technicolor detail. I am so very afraid that I will lose him that I push our relationship to the edges on many occasions, almost as a test to see if he will stick around. If he does, I am relieved for a little while, at least until the next bout of fear comes along. But if my unconscious plans backfire and he blasts back at me…well, that only goes to show what a totally unlovable human being I am after all, doesn't it? I 'win' either way.

I want far too much from him from the very start and it takes me years to realise that and back off and give him room to breathe. I want him to be everything to me. I want him to parent me as well as to love me like a partner. I want him to make decisions alongside me but I am also so afraid of losing the little control I have and therefore lose a little more of myself. Therefore, I ride roughshod over many of the ideas he has, and soon his ideas stop coming completely.

I expect him to read my mind, to be able to look into my eyes and see exactly what is going on in my head. I expect him to be able to read my body language, to always say the right thing at the right time, and when he doesn't, I immediately presume that he doesn't love me enough. I simply cannot hang on to this sensation of being loved at all. It's as if I need him to prove it to me on a daily basis and I desperately yearn for the intensity of the first few months of our relationship. Day to living isn't proof enough for me that he still loves me and needs me and I drive him to distraction with my insecurities, doubts and fears.

But he never goes away…

Yes, Neil has his own problems, too, which contribute to the marriage being less than idyllic, but hey…this is MY story! Neil will have to write his own and spill his own beans! Most importantly of all, he never goes away. He never leaves me. He never abandons me. He never hits me. He never even insults me. Oh yes, we fight and they can be pretty ferocious verbal fights as well, but he never sinks to the depths of calling me names, he never damages my soul in that way. I wish I could say the same…

He is basically a passive man who retreats into himself over the years we are together because he just can't be all that I want him to be. We both made a huge mistake back at the beginning, which has set the tone for our whole relationship. I wanted him to be everything to me and more, and he really did want to be my knight in shining armour and solve all my problems, but no one human being can do that for another. It is just impossible and we both had unattainable goals; very idealistic and noble goals, but totally unattainable all the same.

But the very fact that Neil stays in my life and provides the stability that I have craved for so much over the years, gives me the room to grow emotionally and the time to sort myself out at my own pace. Many many times I want HIM to help me and to make it all okay, but it is a blessing in disguise that he doesn't even know where to start—although it doesn't feel that way at the time, for sure!

People are meant to be in our lives for definite reasons and Neil's role in my journey is to be my rock and one of the few constant people in my whole life. The one person who knows about my binges, my periods of starvation, the fact that I take laxatives (still), the many times I have stolen (although it takes me a very long time to admit that to him)—he knows it all. He knows me, warts and all, and he still wants to be with me.

Wow…

Even as I write this, I still cannot quite comprehend that commitment he had to me through the eighteen years we were together, but I'm getting there…

The Perfect Mother...

I am twenty-seven years old when I have our first and only child, our beautiful daughter, Catherine Louise. She is so desperately wanted by both of us, especially since I had a miscarriage just the year before and we have waited for this day for so very long. When she is placed in my arms at the end of an exhausting thirty six hour labour and her beautiful blue eyes look up into mine, I feel such a connection deep within that I have never felt before. We touch souls in that delivery room and we have continued to do so ever since.

I have wanted so much to be a mother, not just for the usual maternal reasons, but also to fulfil this deep yearning inside me to 'put things right', as it were. It's as if I want to prove to myself and to the world at large that I can be a better mother than my own mother was to me. I have to put right all the previous wrongs in my life and wipe the slate clean. It is a driving force within me that cannot possibly be resolved, but at the time it is my goal to be the perfect mother.

With that need uppermost in my mind, I forge ahead and inadvertently make motherhood so very difficult for myself. I seem to have a knack of that wherever I go through life, but as yet I have learned no other way to react to life. I seem destined to tread a very rocky path in whatever I choose to do, and true to form, I fall victim to post natal depression almost from the day I arrive home from the hospital. I sink lower and lower by the day as it goes unchecked, simply because I have no idea what is really going on within me. I think it is yet more of the eating disorders made worse by the relentless demands of motherhood, but real depression is taking root within me more each day.

My eating goes haywire again, even more so than usual. My sleeping patterns are all over the place as my nerves are so raw that I wake up at every tiny sound, even when Catherine sleeps through the night and doesn't disturb us. I spend my days riddled with the fear that I am doing it wrong and I place an incredible burden upon myself to 'do it right'. In fact, not just right, but *perfect.* It has to be that way; nothing else will do. No short measures for Catherine...not like there were for me.

I must never, ever, let Catherine feel any of the pain and fear that I must have felt as a baby and so I set myself such incredibly unattainable goals as a mother that I can't help but fail on a daily basis. I know that I was left to cry many times when I was little, and so I hate to hear her crying at all. It's as if

I am somehow abandoning her every time I do it. I have to be there for her ALL the time, give her 100%—no, 110%—and I HAVE to do it all perfectly. Every day I lose a little more of ME in an effort to be all things possible to HER, but I can't let go of this grasp I have on the edges of perfection and it is driving me further into insanity.

Ironically, as I cave in under all the pressure, I end up being the kind of mother I have always been terrified of becoming. I cry an awful lot, I shout at Catherine when she screams at me, I even teeter on the edge of really harming her when the frustration builds up to boiling point and I can no longer cope at all. On the surface I am getting by and doing okay, and no one outside the house would ever suspect that I was living with this mental torture. I am far too proud to ask for help and risk having someone think of me as I think of myself—as a complete and utter failure—and so, as always, I keep quiet.

But when Catherine sleeps, I cry and I eat. The excess food is my only real comfort right now and it numbs my mind sufficiently to quiet the manic voices inside my head for a little while at least, until the effect of the sugar wears off and I come out of my stupor. Of course, there is no way it can never be more than a temporary reprieve, and the despair that I already feel is only compounded as the weight piles on yet again. I am soon several stones heavier than I was before having Catherine. Shame overwhelms me…again.

Neil tries desperately to help me, but I shut him out in a lot of ways as I feel that Catherine is *my* sole responsibility. I fear that other people won't know what to do or how to take care of her properly. They won't know what is at stake. Even her own father won't know. It is a kind of vanity, I know, although an inverted kind, as I never feel good enough to be a proper mother, and I will never be able to live up to the standards I set for myself. It is crazy. *I* am crazy.

In the end I have to crack a little. It is inevitable. I have been sitting on the sofa, sobbing uncontrollably for forty-five minutes whilst Catherine screams in her cot in the bedroom and I can no longer bear to hear her cry. I can no longer be here for her. I have nothing left inside me at all. Nothing left to give. I can no longer function. No longer be here for her. I can never be what I should be to her. I have failed. Somebody else should be here for her, not me. I can no longer be here. No longer be here…

Blackness beckons.

Emptiness.

A bottle of pills.

It would be so damned easy.

An end to it all…

But suddenly an image rips into my mind…an image of a crying baby left in the darkness in her pram, abandoned, alone, with her fingers screwed up into a tiny fist, fighting against the world…

Where did that tremendous spirit go?

How can I even think of leaving Catherine?

I can't give up on either of us now.

I can't leave HER the way that I was left.

I HAVE to find some way to break the chain.

Not just for ME but for HER as well.

I have just contemplated suicide in the most serious way I have ever done. I was so very close to reaching out for that bottle of Paracetemol. I could so easily have done it as well. I was minutes away from choosing death over life. From leaving my own baby because I no longer felt worthy of being her mum, or of even being alive.

Two babies save my life that day.

My beautiful little girl, Catherine.

And me.

******

At last I dare to ask for help again, and this time I am a little more successful. Not entirely, but anything is better than nothing. Thank God that somewhere deep inside I am still that fighter with her tiny screwed up fists, although there are lots of days when I feel far from being a survivor.

I am my own worst enemy in many ways as I always have to put on this brave face when I am confronted with the outside world. So despite the fact that I may have been crying my eyes out and screaming at the universe just minutes before, by the time the Health Visitor arrives I appear to be totally in control and it is hard for her to take my problems as seriously as she should. I sit there telling her that my life is a mess, I am so depressed, I have even contemplated ending it all…but I look so OKAY, I know I do. The house isn't particularly in chaos, Catherine sits there in her bouncy chair, looking well fed and gurgling away as if she hasn't a care in the world, my make up is fixed so that the red rims round my eyes don't show, and all looks well in Anne's world. What else is the Health Visitor supposed to think but that I am exaggerating and that life isn't really as bad as I am painting it? She merely picks up on the fact that Catherine doesn't sleep as well as she could and maybe that is the cause of my 'blues'. She refers Catherine to a clinical psychologist who specialises in infant sleeping disorders. Not really what I was looking for, but I can't complain. It's a start, isn't it? And more than I have had up until now.

The next few months pass by in a haze really. I look back at the many photos we took at the time and I am always amazed to see Catherine looking happy and smiling and contented, and in some photos I am even smiling too! I just don't remember it that way; in fact I barely remember it at all, which is so very sad. I am deep in depression at the time but I simply don't know that what I am experiencing is an illness and I feel it is something I should just 'snap out of'. I should be able to cope with a baby. Other people do, why can't I? I see this as another fundamental flaw in my character, and I pile all the blame onto ME yet again. I never ever give myself a break at all.

Inside I am screaming out for help and I am totally desperate. The psychologist is lovely but she points out that she cannot treat *me*, as Catherine is her patient and I should really seek help for my own problems, but I know that I won't go back to the doctor's again—not yet anyway. I convince myself that if Catherine's sleeping habits are improved then it will be better. I know that lack of sleep is just the tip of the iceberg but it is all I can cope with fixing at the minute.

Many of my days are still a web of self-torture and fear and I take it out on those I love the most, namely Neil and Catherine. I turn into a manic control freak and our lives are made even more rigid than before. I am frightened of so much in life that I desperately try to control every last movement of the people I CAN control. In the meantime I lose more and more of myself, and my own behaviour spins wildly out of control. I eat like crazy—anything and everything, massive great binges. I take laxatives again on a regular basis. I try frantically to make myself sick but I never can. Why is it so easy for other people to be sick? I so wish I could do it too…

I worry and panic from the minute I wake up in the morning until the minute I fall into a fitful sleep. I have bad dreams most nights, nightmares in which I leave Catherine somewhere, or I have forgotten I have an exam and am rushing up to school totally unprepared. I wake up feeling as if I am still in the midst of this panic and it takes me a while to realise that it was only a dream. They seem so very real to me though and it takes me at least half a day to shake off the memory of my fears. They come out at night and haunt me through the day. I never get any peace.

My perfectionism when I am with Catherine gets a lot worse as time goes by. Do I talk to her enough? Am I treating her properly? Will she be okay? Am

I feeding her too much? Or maybe not enough? I am so terrified that she will end up having an eating problem like me, even from this early stage in her life. I am frantic when my ever helpful Health Visitor tells me I had better start watering down her bottle as she is putting on weight a shade too fast. I just couldn't bear to pass this on to her too. She mustn't ever suffer the way I did.

I seem totally incapable of calming myself down or facing life with any kind of faith in myself or in the people around me. I stumble blindly from day to day with no plan, no strategy and no foundation at all. I still lean very closely towards the idea of suicide although I know now that I would never actually go through with any suicidal thoughts I might have. But when I am in this self-destruct mode I am even more fearful than usual as there are no boundaries at all to this side of me. There is nothing that I wouldn't say or do to hurt both myself or those I love, and I have no idea just what I may be capable of.

I am a loose cannon when this part of my character has a hold on me and these days are the ones where I simply want to curl up and be little again. I don't want to be the grown-up at all…

The Mum I Call Nanna…

After we get married and move up to Scotland, I see Nanna about eight times a year in all. She just loves coming up to Scotland to stay with us and we try to get down to see her as often as we can, depending on Neil's work and our finances. What a huge support she is to me now and our relationship has really deepened since I got married and even more so since I had Catherine. We can share all kinds of experiences now, and I can appreciate a lot more of what she went through and what she gave up for me, now that I am a mother myself. I also appreciate just how devastated she must have felt when she lost Granpa and a lot of her mood swings and outbursts of anger from that period of time make a lot more sense to me now.

Nanna has been able to relax her control over me as well over the past years– she had no choice really seeing as I moved 300 miles away! But there is a distinct difference in the way she relates to me today. It is as if she has heaved this huge sigh of relief to see me happily married and settled with a child of my own. Maybe she has been able to let go of the fear she had that my life was going to be as dysfunctional as her own children's had been. Her unwavering control over me as I was growing up was really the only way she knew how to protect me from the pitfalls of life, although I managed to find plenty of my own without even really looking.

Still, she sees me happy with Neil now and with a beautiful baby and she is so proud that life has turned out that way for me. She only knows half the story, of course, as we never talk about my eating problems or my depression. I would never want to worry her by letting her know the extent of my troubles and so I get out my brave face again and I never show her the true depth of my despair.

Nanna simply adores Catherine and calls her a 'little beauty'. She loves her to pieces and spoils her rotten like only a Nanna can. It means so much to me that they have such a close relationship, especially seeing as I feel so very awkward when we go down to visit and Catherine spends time with my mum. I resent my mother having anything to do with Catherine most times. I feel that she has no right to be her Grandma in many ways as she was never a mother to me, but I try to put these feelings to one side as much as I can and keep the peace as always. These hostile, resentful feelings towards my mother last for a long, long time though and are never really resolved, even to this day. Too much went unspoken for far too long for us to be close.

But I have Nanna, *we* have Nanna, and she is so wonderful to us. She takes such an interest in our lives, and I have a true feeling of sharing my life with someone who really cares and to whom I really matter. We write to each other two or three times a week, we call each other and we have long chats about our days. When she comes up to stay we have lovely long walks along the beach, we collect shells and paddle together, and we have ice creams and strawberry tarts whilst sitting in the sunshine in the castle grounds. We play endless games of Scrabble, we look at old photos and talk for hours about the past—not MY past, but Nanna's past; her stories from the war, or back when she first met Granpa. The times we spend together are the best we have ever had and I treasure each moment of her visits with us. When she leaves to go home or when the time comes for us to drive away from her house, I feel such a sense of loss that it takes me a full day or more to get used to life without her again. Her spirit fills the house and without it I feel empty somehow until I can pick up the pieces of my routine again and carry on as 'normal'.

When Catherine is around three years old Nanna's health begins to noticeably deteriorate. She is eighty-six years old now, but she has always been so tough, so strong and always there for everyone else, that I never think of her as being old, or even as being a mere mortal. She is my Nanna, always there and always will be.

But she has a series of falls and mini strokes and soon she cannot walk very far. She used to be able to out walk us all and it was a family joke that we would have to slow her down when we were out for a so-called leisurely walk as she set off as if she were on a route march! But now she has to borrow a wheelchair from the Social Services just to get around when she goes out as she can only just manage to potter a few steps around the house.

Nothing stops her from getting on that train to come and see us though. Her spirit is indomitable, and her determination to keep living her life is immense. She comes up in her wheelchair, we take her out as usual, she even goes on the swings in the park on her eighty-seventh birthday! She is amazing. I hate to see her looking so frail now though, and I am reminded every time that we see her that one day it will be for the last time. I start to gather together all my memories of her, just like the beautiful shells that we collected on the beach.

Every minute we spend together is precious now and I try to get down to visit her as often as I can. It's not often enough though as I am now taking care of another young baby on a full time basis too, in order to make a little extra money, as well as looking after Catherine and trying to maintain some level of sanity. The sanity part usually goes by the wayside as I just have too much else going on in my life right now to even give myself space to breathe. My only relaxation is, as always, the food.

******

The following September we arrange a surprise visit to Nanna's, Catherine and I. Nanna isn't doing too well and we arrange with Aunty to arrive on the Friday and just show up on the doorstep. I want to see the look on Nanna's face—we have done this before and it is priceless. I just love to turn up out of the blue.

I phone Nanna as I usually do on the Wednesday evening but there is no reply, which is strange as she is always there. I call around the family and eventually I manage to talk to my cousin, Julie, who tells me that Nanna is in the hospital. She had a very bad fall through the night yesterday and hit her head on the tiled fireplace downstairs. Aunty found her just lying on the floor when she went to make her breakfast that morning. God knows how long she had lain there or what thoughts had been running through her head. Poor poor Nanna…

Our trip down to see her seems even more special now and I still decide to keep it a surprise. Heaven knows why, but I do. I send Nanna a card, my love, a letter and everything possible to let her know that we love her and that we are thinking of her. We are due to arrive there on the Friday evening and we will go straight to the hospital…

…But it isn't to be.

On Thursday evening I am cooking the tea when the telephone rings. I answer it and hear my Aunty's voice on the other end of the line. Immediately I know that something is wrong—she is calling at peak rate time and we only ever call each other through the evenings when it is cheap. What silly thoughts pass through your mind at times like this…

Nanna has died.

At five-twenty—just half an hour ago.

Nanna has died.

Nanna has died…

My mind shuts down completely as if a huge wall has come crashing down between me and all the emotions that threaten to engulf me. I remember letting go of the phone and screaming NO! NO! but almost as if I am on automatic pilot. I know that I am meant to respond that way and I am aware that a bit of me has closed down completely and is watching the rest of me act out this nightmare of a role.

Then I am shot into overdrive and I cannot stop *doing.* I call up my Mum. I go up to see my cousin, Joanne, who lives a few yards up the street from us now, and I comfort her too. I make out a list of people that I need to tell—or rather people that Neil will call for me, as I know I will never be able to get those awful words out in a phone call. I organise myself senseless for hours and never allow myself to stop for fear of having to really feel what is happening. I get out all the photographs of Nanna that I possess and I make them up into an album of just HER and then I feel guilty as if I have taken her away from her family and I want to take them all out again. I sort all her letters into order, hundreds of them.

I just cannot and WILL not stop.

I simply can't be without her. How can I carry on without her? I never want to be without her. I MATTERED to her, really mattered and without her I feel as if I will never matter the same to anyone else again. Not even Neil and Catherine. If Nanna has gone then a huge part of me has gone too.

She took me in, she adopted me, she saved me, she brought me up, she was MORE than a mother to me, she was everything. Even through the years when we weren't close at all I still clung to her with a fierce dependence, as she was the only really strong character in my life. I desperately needed her approval in all that I did, I needed to know that I was good enough for her, and now she has gone. I just cannot comprehend that fact. How will life BE without her? What is the point of doing anything good in my life if she is no longer here to see it? If I can't call her up and share my happiness with her, or tell her my troubles, what is the point?

My mind is awash with questions. Where is she now? Is she okay? Is she in pain? Was she afraid when she died? Did she think that I didn't care because we didn't come down to see her the minute we heard that she was in hospital? I am in a total frenzy and I spin on a merry-go-round of even more pain and fear. My world has turned completely black.

I keep going somehow because I have to for Catherine's sake. She has lost *her* Nanna too. But now, more than ever, I simply do not care what I do to myself. Once again, food is there as my eternal comfort and support and what does it matter how much I eat now anyway? What does anything matter? I can't bring her back…

And so I eat…

One Door Closes…

It seems strange to say but Nanna's death actually marks a huge turning point in my recovery from the multitude of eating disorders and the underlying depression I have lived with for so many years. A subtle change occurs in me from that day onwards, which I cannot even recognise at the time, as I am consumed by grief as well as the ever-present fear and self-loathing that is my life. But looking back, I can see that something was awakened in me and I know exactly the moment it happened.

Catherine and I get the train down to my home town on the Friday as we intended to, but we travel on an earlier train than planned. I learn a very big lesson from that in itself. When I first heard that Nanna was in hospital I just didn't feel able to drop all my responsibilities and go straight down to see her for fear of what others would think of me. But now that it is too late I realise that she was far more important than any job could ever be. I vow that I will never put obstacles like that in the way of the people I love ever again. I should have been there with her. I *could* have been, but I didn't want to let other people down and in the end I feel I have let down the person who meant the world to me.

As soon as we arrive at home I want to see Nanna. I just HAVE to see her. I call up the undertakers and arrange for them to open up especially for me the following afternoon so that I can see her as soon as possible. Why couldn't I have been driven by this desperation when she was still alive?

What I find in that funeral parlour the next day, in that small room where her coffin is lying, shakes my very foundation to the core. I see a body inside that coffin, a stone cold lifeless body, which vaguely resembles the beautiful lady I loved, that I *still* love. I touch her hands and shrink at the texture of her ice-cold skin—hands that have held me, hit me, worked and cared for me. All of those things and much much more. I touch her silver hair—hair that I have cut and played with and brushed. I see the rainbow coloured bruising on her forehead where she fell and hit the fireplace just three days before and I see her lips—flat, thin and lifeless. Lips that kissed me goodnight, shouted at me and talked to me, sang to me and shared secrets with me, and which are now closed forever with a thin line of dried blood between them.

I am crying continuously without even realising I have started and I repeat over and over to her out loud; "It's not you in there, it's not you, it's not you..."

I know that the wonderful human being who was my Nanna just has to be somewhere else. This body is not her. She was so much more than this mere shell and the real Nanna just has to be somewhere else.

The ten minutes I spend in that small dimly lit room beside the body of the lady who took me in and brought me up and loved me the only way she knew how, open up a part of me deep inside that has been closed tightly all my life. I can't see it at the time but there is a definite shift inside me.

I am now ready to learn, ready to listen, REALLY listen to my heart and soul. I become more open minded, and a deep sense of spirituality has entered my being. Not religion, never religion, but an intense faith in the fact that there is more in this world and inside me than I ever dreamed there could be. At last I am ready to find some answers, and what's more, I am ready to act upon those answers and to take responsibility for my own life and happiness, which I have never been willing and able to do before.

Oh, it will still take me years to reach a point where I actually LIKE myself and feel comfortable living in my own skin. But at last I have opened a door marked EXIT and if I am only brave enough to walk through it, I can begin to fight my way out of this nightmare.

Nanna will never ever stop being a big part of my life. I think about her every day and will never forget what she did for me and the lessons she taught me in her own unique way. Even at the end of her life she gave me the greatest lesson of all—that I am more than just this shell that has to be fed and watered to keep it alive. I am more than the outer layer that everyone can see. I have a depth and a soul and a reason to be here on this earth, and I am determined from this moment on that I am going to find it, no matter how long it takes me.

Good night, Nanna, and thank you from the bottom of my heart for all you have done for those you loved. Sleep tight with the angels… Night, night.

Waking Up At Last…

Wow, waking up is certainly a scary process! Not just the opening of your eyes in a morning and facing a new day, but taking the blinkers off your whole life and facing a new way of BEING. It takes more courage that I ever knew I possessed and many times I want to run away and have no further part in this incredibly difficult recovery process. Most days it is easier and far less painful to stay sleepily oblivious to the whys and wherefores that have brought you to this point in your life. I mean, why face up to all the trauma you have been through if you can possibly keep on sweeping it under the carpet and pretending it doesn't exist? That was my family's dogma, after all. Avoid mentioning all these huge events in our lives, pretend they never happened, just carry on as normal, whatever normal was in our family. Lock away the pain and the fear in a dark corner of your mind where you never go and hope that it rots away on its own.

But it never does go away—no, it stays very much alive and thriving, and instead YOU rot away; your soul, your spirit, your spark, your life-force shrivels away until you really DO become the Nothing that you suspect you really are.

It takes me almost forty years to wake up and to live in a way in which I can have moments of complete clarity and absolute connection to the world around me and to the person inside me. And even then I have days when I slip back into the grey soup again. Forty long and painful years, it takes.

But, my goodness, it is well worth every terrified step of the way to stand where I stand today. I wouldn't go as far as to say I would go through it all again—no way! But if that is the journey I had to take to lead me to the joy that I am able to experience right now, then I am truly grateful for all the harsh lessons life has thrown at me.

I am grateful that I am now lucky enough to be able to understand some of the lessons I have been given in this lifetime. I am also very grateful that I now have at least *some* idea of what I need to do in order to lead a really authentic life as ME, instead of always being on the fringes of my existence looking in at myself through frosted glass. I have taken a huge step forwards, faced my fears and lived to tell the tale!

I feel so very lucky to be alive today and I know in my heart that if it can happen to me, then it can happen to any one of you out there as well, whatever you are going through. There is always one defining moment in our lives where the light is switched on inside us and we can see so clearly where we need to go next and what it has all been about. We then have the choice to continue sitting rigid exactly where we are and never attempt to get out of the dark hole we have fallen into over the years. Or we can take a very deep breath and go out there and fight the demons to the best of our abilities.

It will never be an easy choice, but we need to see that we DO have a choice and we also have the power within us to face it, no matter how little we think of ourselves. All we ever need to do is take tiny little baby steps forwards and one day we will look back and we will see that we have walked for miles…

My moment of clarity came in that small room at the undertakers; yours will be totally different again. It doesn't matter when and it doesn't matter where it happens, just as long as it *does*. I was never the same person again after that, not exactly the same anyway. A spark had been lit inside me. Something had changed and a new strength was growing within me minute by minute. It marked the beginning of my time to move on, my time to recover, and my time to be the person I was always meant to be…

This is the message I want to shout out so very loudly as I reach the part in my story where my life DOES start to improve. No matter *how* desperate our lives become, no matter how much pain and fear we have to face for whatever reasons, there is ALWAYS a way out, always.

For each and every one of us…

Keep that thought close to your heart as you read on, won't you?

Chapter Five
The Door Marked "Exit"

My Name is Anne...

"Hello. My name is Anne and I am a Compulsive Overeater."

I can't believe I have just said these words—out loud, and in front of a roomful of complete strangers no less. I can't believe that I have actually taken such a huge step in even coming here to this meeting, never mind daring to give my eating habits a title and actually admitting that this crazy behaviour of mine haunts my every waking moment. I am a Compulsive Overeater. That is what I do. That is who I am.

And I am here today for help, to find out where to go next and how to escape this obsessive behaviour that has been such a huge part of my life for the past twenty years or more. I am preparing to face my fears, bare my soul and open myself up to all of the risks I have hidden well away from throughout my life—the ridicule, the rejection, the abandonment—all of that and more. I am standing up here and telling these people just who I am and what I do, and I have absolutely no idea what their reactions will be, but the truth is that I have nowhere else to go now and I need to move forward. I *have* to move forward. My life and my sanity depend on it.

I first saw the advert for this meeting on the library notice board in the town. I wasn't even looking for help that day, I was just browsing through the posters and this particular one leapt right out at me. It was for Overeaters Anonymous—even the name makes me cringe when I say it to myself. I simply hate to admit that is what I do, and I wish it were hidden behind some pretty name instead. Or at least a name that takes away the guilt and changes it into a blameless act...

Anyway, somebody wants to set up an Overeaters Anonymous group here in my town. Is anyone out there interested, the poster asks? I have never even heard of the group before, but I know a little about Alcoholics Anonymous and it is run along the same lines, and besides, there are no other Eating Disorders groups here within a sixty-mile radius, so what have I got to lose?

I decide to pluck up all the courage I possess and go along to that first meeting.

******

"Would you like to tell us a little about yourself?" asks one of the girls there, Audrey, and I can feel myself blushing furiously as all eyes in the room are focused upon me. I have never liked being the centre of attention, and have always tried to divert it right away from me but now it is all mine and I feel incredibly uncomfortable. Audrey must sense my unease as she adds;

"You don't have to speak, of course, No one here does. We are all here to say what we want and to listen when we feel we cannot talk. You will never have to say anything you don't want to. Just listen for now if you'd prefer. It's really okay"

But I know in my heart that if I don't open my mouth and speak here and now then I most probably won't even have the guts to come back to the next meeting. I will run away and hide as I have done so many times in the past. There comes a time when although every last instinct inside you screams at you to run, your very soul knows that you need to stay and face the demons instead.

So, here goes…very deep breaths, and a whole heap of courage. Don't look at anyone, look at the floor, the walls, anywhere but in people's eyes. I can't face looking into someone's eyes. Or maybe I just don't want them to see into mine…

"My name is Anne and I am thirty-four years old. I have had problems with my eating for as long as I can remember and I really need help to get through this."

My God, this is harder than I thought it would be. How many times in my life have I said those words out loud. *I need help*. Wow…I can't believe I am doing this. And still there is a warm and comforting silence in the room and still they are listening to me. No one has turned away. No one is laughing. It is safe to carry on.

"I am married to Neil, I have a daughter called Catherine and I am making their lives a living Hell with my need to control everything that goes on around me. I have to do something to change the way I act before I lose all that is good in my life. But I just don't know what to do. I have absolutely no idea where to start."

I pause and fiddle with my wedding ring, and fight off this sudden urge to cry. I could never allow myself to cry in front of someone else, not like this anyway, and so I swallow the lump in my throat and regain my composure before I try to continue. But I don't know what else to say? There is so much…all those years of pain and fear. How can I possibly fit them into a few minutes? How can I even begin to put it into words?

But what I don't realise is that I really don't even need to try. Every single one of the people in this room today has been where I have been and where I still am. I don't need words to explain to them what it is like to be me. They know what the obsession with food is like, they have stood firmly in my shoes, and they can identify so well with even the few words that I can say.

In that small room that day I find such acceptance and understanding, beyond my wildest dreams. After that one meeting I know that here is a place I can come and no one will ever laugh at me, no one will judge me, no one will ever hurt me or treat me badly. We are all here for the same reasons—to learn how to live sanely in a world which has become totally crazy for us over the years. We are all learning how to cope with life on a daily basis without the emotional crutch of food to cling onto. It is an absolute revelation to me and I feel as if I have come home at last.

In front of this group of people that I have never met before in my life, I can stand up and say;

"I can't do this alone. I need help."

And that is the biggest step forward I have ever taken.

******

It means the world and more to have another human being know exactly what you are talking about when you say you just HAD to eat that apple pie or you would have gone crazy. To have someone nod with compassion when you say that you swallowed a whole pack of laxatives today because you just HAD to get rid of the food in your system is an absolute gift. And, it is an even greater gift to be able to give that compassion right back to someone else who is suffering. To be able to listen to another person's pain and be able to say, I know just what you mean, and REALLY know what she is saying and feel it in your very soul, opens doors inside that let so much goodness flow into your being.

There are many organisations out there in the world, many websites, many self-help groups, many professional programmes—all there with the aim of helping people overcome their Eating Disorders. It may be that you don't find the right one for you first time, but never ever give up looking. You are far too important for that. Far too deserving of help and peace of mind.

The same goes for any addiction or problem in life. Finding that all-important identification with another 'sufferer' is so much of a lifeline along the road to recovery. Knowing that it isn't just YOU, knowing that there are thousands of people out there who feel exactly the same way that you do—well, words can't quite explain the flood of relief that it brings. Knowing that you have a safe place you can go every week and be able to open up and say whatever you want and still be accepted for who you are…knowing that no one will think you are greedy and disgusting and revolting and all those labels you pin onto yourself on a daily basis. Instead they will see you as a wounded human being who needs love and support, just as you see them, and you will begin to feel that maybe, just maybe, you are okay after all.

There is no shame in asking for help. None at all. Our pride sometimes gets in the way or else we feel we are totally undeserving of help but that is so very far from the truth. Imagine yourself as somebody else. If you came across someone else who was suffering in the way that you are, you would reach out and help them immediately, wouldn't you? You wouldn't even need to think twice about it. So why not allow yourself to receive that same love and compassion from somebody else, and ultimately from yourself?

And please don't give up if the first person you tell doesn't respond the way you would like. It just means you have found the wrong person to share your problems with at that time and that there are far more understanding people out there—you just need to keep on looking. Overeaters Anonymous wasn't the first self-help group I went to, but it was the right one for me at the time, and I am so very glad that I kept on looking otherwise I just wouldn't be where I am today.

******

I go home after that first meeting having said little more about myself but I have done a whole lot of listening and I know that this is the right place for me to be at this point in my life. I am ready to give more of myself, ready to reach out for help, and ready to open myself up and look for answers, however painful a task it may be. After all, how can it possibly be any more painful that what I have endured over the years? It is just the fact that moving forward is unknown and we always prefer a fear and a pain that we know to one that we don't. But now it is time and I am ready…

It feels as if something has opened up within me after that first meeting and I start to write and write as soon as I have the free time. Words are pouring out of me so fast that I can't write them down quickly enough—feelings, fears, anger,—it all comes out in black and white and I am amazed by the depth of emotion within me. All this has been shut away for so long. Where did I keep it all? What was it doing to me? How was I able to hide all this and still manage to live?

I write and write until I am exhausted and then I put down my pen and I sleep; a peaceful, dreamless sleep for hours on end. Oh, there is such a long way to go, I know, and so much more to pour out of me, but for the first time ever I feel as if I have taken hold of the reins of my life and it is ME who is deciding which way to go next.

Wow…what an incredible sensation…

A Silent Vow

A silent vow unto myself
To change the way I live my life,
The way I hide away from life
Behind all these pitiful excuses—
Too fat, too old, too everything.

For time goes much too fast to hide away,
Too fast to wait upon perfection.
I have to cast my fears aside
And find change before it is too late,
Before all I have are countless diaries
Filled with wasted years and many tears.

I must learn to live my life again
And find myself
And BE myself
And love myself.

So Very Little To Do With Food…

Do you know, I always though it was about the food and the weight and nothing else? All my life I have believed I have *eating* problems, with names such as anorexia, bulimia, and compulsive overeating. There is no doubt in my mind that I DID suffer from these illnesses, but they were merely the tip of the iceberg and by no means the whole story. Underneath the starving and the bingeing there lies an entire volcano of smothered emotions. Times when I have had to stuff the feelings away inside rather than let them out and express how I feel. The times I was never allowed to speak, never allowed to ask questions. The doubts, the insecurities, the fears that I could never put names to, the screams I held inside for fear of rocking the boat and upsetting somebody else. The pain that I hid because I didn't want people to think badly of me. Oh, the list is endless.

It is all there, locked away beneath this facade of multiple eating disorders and only now do I see with such clarity that in order to release the need to overeat and starve or binge and take laxatives, I need to deal with each and every one of these feelings as I should have been allowed to deal with them way back then. What an enormous and terrifying task. But with the support of my new friends at OA, I don't have to face any of this alone now. They are at the end of a phone, day or night, and all I need to do is ask for help.

At the meetings it surprises me that we barely talk about the food issues in our lives. I imagined we would sit there and 'confess' to eating three packets of biscuits for breakfast, six Mars bars for lunch, or whatever and then we'd sympathise with each other and say yes, we understand. But it is nothing like that at all. We're not here to focus on our *food* problems but on our *life* problems, our *coping* problems, and the food barely ever gets mentioned.

This is a whole new way of thinking for me, a real revelation. I have always believed that if I could just lose weight, then everything around me would be fine. My life would be perfect and what's more, *I* would be perfect too. It all boiled down to calorie lists and exercise as far as I was concerned, but now I see that it goes way deeper than that. I have the power within me to *really* change my life and it has absolutely nothing to do with calories and food charts and walking for miles in the blazing sun. Instead it is all about changing my attitudes, changing the way I react to situations that are out of my control, the way I let people take advantage of me, the way I seem determined that everybody else is far more important than I am, the way that I choose to live my life, and the way that I choose to BE.

I can change all that, it seems. Other people in this group have done it. They tell me their stories and I am amazed. I never thought I could have that power in my life, but if they can do it and they were once where I am now, then maybe I can do it too.

This is enormous.
I am overwhelmed with the possibilities that lie ahead.
I can be free, if I just choose to be free.
Wow...

But first I need to do a whole lot of work. Write it all down, they tell me. Get it out onto paper. Tell your story. See it for yourself. See it in black and white and really try to understand where you have been for the first time ever. Only then can you really see where you may be going.

And so, I make sure that I find the time to write every day. I find the strength and the courage to write and I let myself go and wait to see just what comes out...

And the words you will read next are what came tumbling out...My first attempt to find ME.

Scared Inside My Skin...

Today is one of those days where I just can't sit still—where I have to keep busy, keep my mind active, because if I dare to stop, then the 'Unease' takes over. That unnamed fear that haunts me day and night, and if that happens I have nowhere to left run because the fear is in me, the fear IS me and I cannot escape.

I guess to the vast majority of the human race that I encounter, I'm just an ordinary person who copes with life pretty well. I am married, I have one happy, healthy young daughter, and I hold down a job as a Sales Assistant at the local University. I always dress fairly neatly, I'm never seen outside the house without my make-up neatly done (God forbid!) and I'm pleasant and polite to everyone.

But inside I seethe. I seethe with anger, resentment, fear, pity, panic, self-doubt—in fact, I seethe with just about every negative emotion you can think of. These feelings don't always manifest themselves as words or actual thoughts in my head, but they exist more as a creeping mass of feelings which engulf me some days, and I end up feeling so trapped inside myself that I could scream.

But I don't—because I am a born Coper. And Copers don't scream to get attention and help for themselves. Copers just get on with life and suffer in silence, or at least silence as far as the outside world is concerned. My long-suffering husband and daughter would dearly relish a little silence from me some days, as to them I tend to openly seethe. To them I can be hateful and hurtful and picky and angry and very much a control freak. My life seems so topsy turvy to me some days that I simply *have* to control someone or something and, as I'm basically afraid of the world and his mother, the ones who are closest to me bear the brunt of my fears. Actually, my external life isn't topsy-turvy at all; it's quite normal and I am relatively safe and settled with no threats to my existence or my sanity, at least none from the outside. It all comes very much from within.

And sometimes that can actually be a relief—to know that it's just ME who's a little crazy and that the rest of the world is basically okay (give or take a few terrorists, religious fanatics, despots and mass murderers!). It's a huge relief to know it's 'only' ME that I have to change and the rest of the world can go about its business, and that I'm not responsible for the actions of a single one of them. It's an enormous relief to know that everyone ISN'T out to get me, although it certainly seems that way at times to Little Miss Paranoid here!

On the other hand, wouldn't it be great if I could simply say;

"If only so-and-so would change his or her behaviour I would be happy" or

"If only my work hours were different I would be a far more settled person"

What it boils down to is this; if only I could alter the world to be exactly as I would want it to be, then I would intrinsically be okay. Except that I know I wouldn't, because I would still be left with the scary menagerie of thoughts and feelings that is me.

And so I recognise that I need to work on ME. But that's not anywhere near as easy as it sounds. Where do I start? What do I do if I find that ultimately I *can't* live with myself, or I can't change myself? Do I have to keep on living in this purgatory forever? Do I have to endure a lifetime of being afraid of myself and who I am, and so uncomfortable in my own skin that it almost feels like an alien? I feel like I have someone else's kidney inside me that I'm constantly rejecting, except that this metaphorical kidney is the whole entire ME.

Maybe I was given the wrong body at birth, the wrong parents, the wrong life! Whatever it is, I have always felt as if I was on the edge of my life waiting to be invited in, except that no-one would, and I was far too scared to invite myself in for fear of rejection.

Food has always been my dearest friend and my cruellest enemy. I turned to food from the time I could do an 'Oliver' and ask for more, and I turned to it with a passion, an obsession that is akin to a drug addict with his heroin. I have always had this gaping hole inside of me and food was a very good temporary 'bung' to this hole. It never lasted, of course, and I then had the added problem of further isolating myself because of being overweight and having even less confidence. Even as I write this, I am thinking of the Snickers bars in my fridge and I may well succumb to temptation just to shut that voice up for even a short while.

Food replaces love and a feeling of being wanted. Rejection by my parents as a baby has left deep mental scars and I am sure that somewhere, deep within my being, I feel that if THEY couldn't love me and want me, then I am totally worthless and no-one will love and want me. Then, like a small child cutting off its nose to spite its face, I set out to prove it. I overeat. I make myself fat, and then I can triumphantly say;

"There, see! It's true! No one DOES want me!"

I convince myself that I can't join in the world completely because I am fat and, therefore, unacceptable, whereas what I really feel is far deeper inside and far more painful. I don't really feel unacceptable because I am fat—I feel unacceptable because I am ME.

This is such a tremendously intense feeling that I can't handle it—I have to turn it into something tangible that I CAN understand. So I overeat compulsively and then I can see fat upon myself, which I personally find unacceptable and everything becomes relatively easier to deal with.

—There, see! I went and ate the three Snickers bars after all, and now the voice inside my head is quieted for a while and instead I can concentrate on how physically uncomfortable I feel. How bloated, how sick, how hot and how gross and ugly I am. When I can no longer cope with the mental trauma that is constantly raging inside myself, I turn it into a physical problem, which, if not exactly easy to deal with, is at least tangible, and far more black and white. I eat compulsively, therefore I feel fat and ugly. X = Y. It's all so much easier to comprehend that way.

Sometimes I hate myself so much that I want to hurt myself physically. It doesn't matter how awful I'll feel if I eat all that food. I don't care if I feel sick—in fact sometimes I'd just *love* to be sick, except the sane, rational side of me has always detested being sick and in that area at least sanity reigns and I have never been able to make myself sick after a binge. However, I have used laxatives on many, many occasions, which seems kind of ironic when I think about it. I overeat to fill the cavern inside me then I yearn so desperately to be empty again that I purge myself in an awful and painful way. I cause myself embarrassment and humiliation, having in the past been badly affected by overdoses of laxatives whilst at work or outdoors. It is simply hellish, but I still do it…

No normal, sane human being would put themselves through that, surely? But then I have this reckless part of me that just doesn't care, and I would go even further and say that this part of me actually rejoices in the pain and discomfort because…well, I'm not sure why. Maybe I like the way I can control my own body (although I blatantly cannot). No one else can do this to me and cause this much turmoil within me physically when I binge or purge or starve. Again, it's as if my body isn't really ME, like I've always disowned it and done what I can to destroy it without daring to take that one very final path of destruction and actually kill myself.

I have also hurt myself in other ways—burnt myself with scalding water, scratched myself with needles enough to draw blood and leave temporary scars. I have taken mild overdoses of medicine because I wanted to be unconscious and not have to think, and as I mentioned before, I have badly denied myself food. I have existed on 200 calories a day at times, and once I ate nothing at all for eight days in a row. Black coffee and sugar free gum were all that passed my lips for eight whole days.

I wish I could have even just a little more regard for myself today. I want so strongly for my daughter to grow up with a deep sense of self-worth that I say to her all the things that I wish somebody had said to me when I was young. I wanted to hear them often enough for me to believe them and for them to become embedded deep inside my soul. If only someone had told me when I was five or six or seven that I was a worthwhile human being, that it didn't matter what I did in my life, I would always be loved unconditionally. I would always be accepted for whatever I did as I grew up and whoever I became, that I'd always have a home where I'd be safe and wanted, would I be sitting here writing all this today? Perhaps those Snickers bars would still be in the fridge, too? Who knows?

Now when words like that are said to me, they hit a solid brick wall and mean very little. My husband has told me for many years that he loves me and thinks I am pretty and special and worthwhile, and although I think I almost believe him on an intellectual level, deep within those words fall into a bottomless pit and disappear. They barely even touch me at all. Love falls through me and it slips out of my grasp every time.

Looking back, I think that the anorexic period of my life was a rather twisted stand for freedom amongst other things. An effort to break out of a very claustrophobic family where I never felt valued as a person, but rather for the promise of what I would become and what I could achieve academically. I was very bright with excellent school reports and people expected great things of me. When exams came around, I was simply expected to perform well and all expressions of doubt on my part were cast aside as if they were saying; "How can you possibly think you won't pass when we are 100% certain that you will?"

I lived with that pressure always—at home and at school, so in the end I lived as I was expected to live and the doubts and the fears went inside and became part of this creeping mass of fear that has always been lurking somewhere deep within.

So I struck out. I rebelled in the only way I knew how. I was a 'good girl' and I felt that I couldn't rebel outwardly, so I took it all out on myself. Everything else in my life seemed out of control and I grasped the only control I could—over my own body. Except I was never really in control at all, was I? Oh yes, I could tot up the calories and write out constant charts and plot my weight loss on graphs and wait for the time when I would hit that magic 'right' figure on the scales; when all would be perfect in my life. Except it never was, was it? Maybe another half a stone would do the trick, but no, so I'd go for another and another, whilst all along I lived with the terror that it was never going to be right and this wasn't the answer. But I was stuck on this conveyor belt of starvation and denial and there seemed no sane, rational way to escape it.

So I took an insane, irrational way out…and literally overnight, I started to binge and purge myself. After that I was *totally* out of control and it felt as if my eating mirrored my whole life. I stopped studying properly at school and only just scraped by in my 'A' levels. I gave up all my hopes of going to University (or had they ever been MY hopes?) and I became a big hopeless failure. But, when I look back, twenty years later, on this period of my life, I wonder if indeed the bulimia was my true strike for freedom. It certainly put an end to everyone else's expectations of me and, although I was bingeing heavily, I was now so very aware of the huge void in my life, which I hadn't consciously been before. Once I let go of acting like I believed I was expected to, what was there left but a big, huge Nothing, and that was what I physically became.

And years later I'm still trying to fill that hole and become a complete human being, whatever that may be. As I am learning more about myself and my compulsions, I am trying to fill the hole emotionally and nurture myself in other ways rather than constantly feeding myself, but nothing seems to work on a permanent basis. I can have a reasonably good day by myself and then the minute I tell my husband or daughter about it, I feel as if all the emotional stability I have built up throughout the day has gone and I'm back to feeling all needy and vulnerable and resentful again. It's like I've given my day, and therefore myself, away to them and I have nothing left inside me.

I resent my husband for not taking care of me the way that I, irrationally, feel I should be taken care of. Basically I want him to parent me, but then the freedom fighter in me wouldn't stand for anyone dominating me in any way. It's like I can never win and HE certainly can never win! I have so little reserves of my own that those I do have are so easily dispersed and I then need so much from others that I am constantly disappointed and dejected when they cannot come up with the goods.

And so I eat. It's an awful lot easier to have an eating problem than a life problem. Easier to be scared of a piece of apple pie lurking in the fridge because of the perceived power it has over you than to be afraid of your very soul because of its powerlessness. Better to be full of food than empty of love.

Sounds dramatic? Well, that's the way it is. I can be standing ironing a shirt or something and I will look absolutely normal, but my mind is actually in turmoil;

"What can I eat now? No, I shouldn't have that, but I really want it. I could maybe have it if I go for a long walk or do thirty sit-ups afterwards—except I'll feel so rotten then I won't be able to move. I know I could take some laxatives, but then I'm out in the morning and won't be near a toilet…"

And so it goes on…or my tirade could be more on an emotional level;

"How can I carry on needing so much and feeling constantly let down? Is it fair of me to expect others to live around me in this way? Could I survive on my own? Do I expect the wrong things from a partnership? I'm sure so-and-so at work doesn't like me. Is it because of my lack of confidence? My looks? My ability or not to do the job?…."

My mind is like a non-stop market researcher, constantly asking questions, but receiving few real answers, and apart from a few minutes of clarity and peace here and there, it is basically only stilled by food and sleep…just like a baby. Have I travelled through all these years of life only to remain where I was at the start? Screaming for food and attention? Desperately needing love?

I know it is up to me to build my own foundations now. The people who should have done it for me all those years ago reneged on the task and no one else in the world can ever take their place, however hard they try. I wanted to really *belong* to someone, to know that I meant more to them than anything else in the world, to be a real part of them, to feel safe and solid and secure. But instead I was neglected and abandoned and grew up feeling like I didn't belong anywhere with anyone.

And now, as I attempt to build upon my daughter's foundation, I have to also find the reserves to build my own, almost from scratch, and it's the hardest task I will ever have to do. I am a thirty-four-year-old woman, but in reality I feel like a very small, frightened child; scared of the world, scared of myself…simply scared within my own skin.

And sometimes, even a Snickers bar can't take that feeling away completely…

Facing the Demons…

I still have those manic voices in my head; the ones that tell me to eat or not to eat. To exercise or to sit down and relax. To starve or to binge. Most days can I fight them for a little while but then I give in because it really is just easier that way. It is always easier to do just as they tell me. That way it is all over and done with and I can carry on as I was …until the next time.

But today I am determined to try and fight them all the way to the very end. I don't know what has inspired this sudden strength within me but I feel that there is just a chance that today I may be able to face up to these demons I have lived in fear of for so very long.

I am absolutely terrified by the prospect though, and right now I feel as if I am standing on the edge of a huge cliff with the waves down below me crashing violently against the rocks and laughing up at me mockingly. It is as if all the fears I have ever had in the world are in those waves and if I don't take refuge in my food as I usually do I will be sucked down into that wild and rocky sea and be lost forever.

The voices start to creep into my head at around nine o'clock this particular night. I am sitting on the settee reading a book, having just got Catherine settled down to sleep. Neil is watching a TV programme but the sound is turned down quite low and the house is almost silent. All seems relaxed…for a little while at least.

But then something palpable shifts inside me and my initial reaction to this physical feeling is as always EAT. I can ignore it at first, as the voice is fairly quiet. But then it starts to be more specific and it tells me in great detail about the chocolate that is left over from Catherine's Christmas selection boxes. It is sitting there in the kitchen cupboard and she has so much of it left that she surely wouldn't miss a couple of bars, would she?

Usually I can resist for a little bit longer these days before I finally give in and walk like a zombie into the kitchen for my 'fix'. I tell myself that no way do I need this, I shouldn't do it, and it is BAD. I'll just feel awful afterwards like I always do. I have done so very well with my food today. How can I spoil it now? But even though I have a hundred and one rational arguments for why I shouldn't give in and start to binge, I am usually overwhelmed by this surge of panic that wells up in me when I try to fight back. I start to shake and feel as I am going to…going to what? What on earth can possibly happen to me if I don't eat?

I will plunge over that cliff, that's what will happen. I will fall into total blackness, total darkness, total madness, and something awful will happen to me, something far worse that I can possibly imagine, even worse than a physical death. It is a fear of this Unknown that usually makes me give in to the voices, and grab the food quickly to quell the terror. At least I know for sure what the excess food will do to me, and what's that old saying? Better the devil you know…at least until tonight.

Tonight I am going to hold my head up high and walk right through those fears and see just what is really on the other side. I want to know just what will happen to me if I don't binge. Because I desperately need to know. This fear is a huge wall that I keep banging my head against day after day before I turn tail and run away once more. If I run to the food every time that fear shows up, then how can I ever dig myself out of this dark hole I inhabit?

I am starting to shake now, imperceptibly at first, but it feels so much worse from the inside. The voices in my head are louder now and they build up to a scream that crashes wildly from side to side inside my skull.

CHOCOLATE!!! CHOCOLATE!!! CHOCOLATE!!!
NOW…NOW…NOW!!!!!!!!!

It is like a manic Mayday call from a pilot who is about to crash onto those rocks below. There is the same terror and intensity in the tone and the same absolute desperation. The voices fill my entire head now and my mind is buzzing with the noise. I need to drown them out. I need to eat.

But I make myself sit rigid on the settee with my book gripped tightly in my hand. I will not move…

I can see myself over and over again, walking into the kitchen, picking out the chocolate I want, unwrapping it carefully, and taking that first sublime bite—God, it would be the answer to all the terror building up inside me right now. It would calm me down immediately, that very fist bite would push away the fear and make everything okay again. I could face just these fears another time, couldn't I? *This* time I could just give in….

NO!!!!!

I am visibly trembling now and I feel so very cold and clammy. My heart is starting to race and I am incredibly jumpy, as if I am steeling myself to be attacked from all sides. The adrenaline is pumping wildly through my body in waves and I am on full alert. Something terrible is going to happen to me, I just know it is. I am going to tipple over the edge, I am going to crash against those rocks and I am going to be torn to pieces. Except I won't die and I will have to live in agony and in mere shards of the human being I once was. It will be like a living Hell. The pain and the fear will be everlasting. I cannot allow myself to fall. I need my safety net NOW!

But still I make myself sit rigidly on that settee and I will not move.

The fear is overwhelming now. I can feel it rising up through my body like a physical entity and I feel as if I am about to drown in it completely. It is a nameless fear, a faceless fear, and all-encompassing fear, something which has no solid base but is a mass of blackness surrounding and smothering my soul. This is what I have been hiding from and for every good reason as well. I would give anything right now to be rid of this fear and get safely back to the pain that I know. I would eat myself to death if it meant I would never have to face this incredible terror again. What is it? Where does it come from? How can I chase it away, other than with food? What can I do? Help me, please…

I have no answers, so for now I stay sitting rigidly on the settee with my book, and the knuckles on my hands are white and my whole body shakes.

Neil asks me what is wrong. Can he get me anything, but I shake my head frantically and he leaves me alone. This can't possibly go on forever. It simply has to subside at some point. The voices in my head have no actual words now, just an awful heart-rending scream that pierces through to my very core and rocks me back and forth on the edge of this cliff of mine.

But I hold on tight, I raise my head, I take many deep breaths and I WILL the fear to subside. I look it square in the eyes, I tell it that I have no idea why it is here with me today but that I am determined to find out why I am so afraid. I am more certain than I have ever been before in my life that one day this fear will not be a huge mass living in my very soul. One day I will be able to walk beside this fear and not let it block my path any more. One day I will be okay and I will live without fear...

Something strange is happening to me now. The voices are quietening a little and the shaking is lessening. I watch and I listen and I observe the changes within me, and very slowly the shaking stops completely, my heart rate slows and I am able to move my tensed up body at last. The fear is dying away...it is crawling back to wherever it came from and I have lived to tell the tale.

I cannot believe it!!! I DIDN'T EAT!!! My God!!!! I didn't give in, I didn't eat!!! I faced up to whatever has driven me to damage myself for years and I am still here...still sitting on this settee with my book in my hands. I am still here.

I cannot believe this has happened...

This is the single most important experience of my whole food-related existence. I didn't eat when I was told to eat. WOW...this is BIG...

Yes, it was awful, it was horrendous and terrifying, but I DID IT!!!

I have chased those demons back into their dark hole without having to squash them down with food. I have used my own strength and power to face up to them and I have won.

If I can do it once, maybe, just maybe, I can do it again? What do you think?

Maybe I have found my door marked 'Exit' at last...

******

The very next time I go to an OA meeting I share this incredible experience with the other girls and they are all so very proud of me that I glow from the inside out. Nowhere else on this earth have I ever found such a depth of understanding and acceptance. Resisting the temptation to eat might seem like such an easy task to someone who has never lived with an eating disorder or an addiction of some kind. Only a person who has faced such a life threatening addition can possibly understand just what an amount of inner strength it takes to face up to the fears behind the addiction and not to grab onto our chosen drug of choice to get us through unscathed.

These girls and the programme of recovery that I find at OA are the tools that eventually open my eyes and allow me to see a real way out of my fear of living. The people with whom I share my fears every week show their total acceptance of me and make me see that I am okay, that I am good enough. In return, I am all too eager to give them the gift of acceptance right back, and we show each other over and over again that is it okay to be US and that we are really pretty damn good human beings.

This is the wonderful message every time that I walk into this small group of people. It is such an important part of my recovery, as are the twelve steps, which are part of every programme of this kind. They give me a path to follow and when I flounder and wonder just what to do next, there is always an answer for me. There is always someone to talk to, always a question to answer to provoke even more soul-searching and the brick wall I have built to protect me from the fear slowly comes down brick by brick.

The girls who have been in recovery for far longer than me are my inspiration. I look at them and instead of thinking, I could never be like them, as I would once have done, I tell myself that one day I will have that serenity as well. One day I will know peace of mind and be comfortable living in my own skin. Every week they give me hope and that is a gift and a half.

Ask yourself questions all the time, Audrey tells me. Dive right into that fear with the faith that you will be okay, whatever happens. You are never alone now. Give your fears a name. Find out what they are saying to you. Why they are there. Where they stem from. If you can give names to your fears then you can deal with them one by one and make your life a whole lot more manageable.

I am more than willing to do whatever Audrey suggests I do, as she has been where I am now and she has come through. She is a survivor for sure. She is happy. She no longer binges. She shows me what I can be if I am willing to put in the work.

And by God, I am willing. What other alternative do I have? More years of pain and depression and fear? No way. Now is my time to break free. I can do it, I know I can…I just need the courage to answer all these questions and face my own truths…

Faith in Today

The world seemed so hostile this morning,
So grey and cold and utterly friendless,
So frightening too, spiralling out of control,
With me hanging there by a thread in the middle,
Spinning round and around, falling down, down, down.

I walked to the castle this morning.
I stood by the sea and was calmed by the waves.
I remembered the people I grew from
And the people I'm growing towards,
And I found I could suddenly raise a smile
And the world slowed right down and was still.

And now my world's full of friends again,
Thanks to time by the sea,
Thanks to you there for me,
Thanks to time out and peaceful remembrance,
Thanks to knowing it will all be okay
If I simply have faith in today...

Question and Answer Time...

And so I sit, with my paper and pen, and a list of questions that Audrey has given me to help direct my thoughts and hopefully dispel a few more demons along the way. The fear is already raising its ugly head and my hand shakes slightly as I begin to write. There is still chocolate up in the kitchen cupboard but I am determined to do this 'cold turkey'. I choose to unwrap some more layers of my incredibly complex self rather than the wrappers on a chocolate bar, and I am so very grateful that I am even capable of making a decision such as that today.

Here goes...honesty time...I look through all the questions, I make notes, I take many deep breaths and this is what I come up with...

Who Am I?...

At thirty-six years old, to be even asking that question seems rather strange! But I honestly have no real idea who I am, or at least I don't think I do. I have spent the vast majority of my life trying to be what I believed other people *wanted* me to be or living up to sometimes imagined, sometimes real, expectations. I always tried to be liked and to gain other people's approval, even if it sometimes meant going against my natural instincts. Gradually those natural instincts simply stopped working and I had to constantly look towards other people to even gauge my own feelings. I ceased to be a whole person within myself, if indeed I had ever been one. Instead I became this mass of fears and insecurities that can so easily be rocked from one extreme to another emotionally, depending on the mood of whoever I happen to encounter on any given day.

Alone, I can feel okay, and I am able to establish an almost stable frame of mind within myself some days. Yet as soon as another person enters the frame my mood switches immediately and the ME I have grown to be whilst alone dissipates and I react so strongly to the other person's mood. I have grown so tired of this constant rising and falling of emotions. So tired of never knowing how I will be from day to day, of hoping that our time spent together as a family will be okay and that I will be able to maintain an even keel and not spoil the time for the people I love. And the result of all this is that I just don't know who I am.

I don't trust myself. It doesn't come naturally to me to take care of myself. I feel thirsty but I hold back from giving myself a drink. I feel cold but I won't put on the fire or another jumper. I know I will feel both mentally and physically bad if I overeat yet I continue to do it. I know that my mental and physical well being has been so low for so long, but still I continue to ignore myself. I read self-help books whilst eating a huge apple pie and shivering with the cold. Where am *I* in all this?

I think the best way to try and get to know myself is to stand outside of myself and see what I would make of 'me' if I were someone else. What would I think of the person I find? Would I want to be my friend? I am writing this on what is, up to now, a fairly 'Good' day, so maybe I will be able to be a little kinder to myself today. It is certainly worth a try!

So…this Anne person…what is she *really* like? The Good and the Bad…but the Good first as I am always an expert at finding the Bad!

Well…she tries to be as kind to other people as she can be and she wants to make a real difference to the world in whatever way she can. Her heart is very much in the right place and her intentions are good, but because she doesn't always look after herself very well, she is often not able to give as much as she would like, or else she burns herself out by giving too much.

She doesn't really care much for the practicalities of life, and the way that things 'should' be done. She would be quite a rebel if she had more confidence to do so! She questions authority but never has the guts to actually do something about it…not yet anyway! She is more of a creative person than a practical one, although the practical things DO get done, just in rather a haphazard way!

She is a great 'people' person. She loves to watch people, to listen to their stories, and to try to get inside their heads and feel what they have felt. Too much, sometimes! She sees everyone as complete human beings rather than as mere two-dimensional shells, and tries as much as possible not to judge others. After all, she is usually far too busy judging herself to spend a lot of time on others' faults! She feels rather uncomfortable with people who hide themselves away (much as *she* does really) as she yearns for honesty and openness and is trying to be much more like that herself. She has hidden away inside herself for far too long.

Despite all the setbacks she has had in her life, there remains an indomitable spark of life inside her, an unsinkable soul that carries her forward even when she doesn't believe there really is a 'forward' to be carried to. She will always look for the way out of despair and will not expect to be handed the solutions on a plate—although it would be wonderful if it happened that way!

She believes intrinsically that all human beings are equal (except once again, herself) and that no one should be considered above anyone else just because of their career status or their colour or religion, and so on. Unfortunately she cannot see her own worth very well and looks to others for her own sense of self and some validity. She does not give up easily on other people, not without a darned good fight, and I suppose that, despite her lack of self-esteem, she has not completely given up on herself either.

She is a deeply spiritual person, but not in a religious way. She believes that organised religion can sometimes be very divisive and damaging in a global way, and she does not conform to any set beliefs. Her own beliefs and principles are growing as she learns more about the world and the way she fits into it through her own experiences and those written by others in books. She is an avid reader and loves words with a passion! She loves the way that words can be used in so many ways to connect people and to make us all feel less alone in the world. She is so very grateful to the people who have been able to put their complex feelings into words so that people like her who are floundering can identify and feel a little less alone.

She is a writer herself, both of poetry and short stories and occasional ramblings of thought! She has this feeling right now that there is so much more inside her just waiting to come out, but that the time is not yet right. One day though…the feelings and the words have to be 'right there' inside her, waiting to bubble out and have real meaning. That is the way she writes, from pure inspiration. Her words cannot be written in any mechanical or practical way. They have to come straight from the soul.

She has an absolute passion for music as well. A wide range of music from the present day charts to some classical pieces, from bouncy catchy tunes to meaningful and melodic songs, from rock to pop. She is quite talented musically herself, although this has been dropped by the wayside over the years and she finds it difficult at present to have the commitment to relearn an instrument. She has this block which makes it hard for her to embark on any project for fear of not being able to carry it through to the end. She has such a fear of failure, but hopefully that will subside as she gains more faith in her own abilities.

She has raised a lot of money for charity over the years, the most successful venture being the thousand pounds she raised for several charities by selling homemade salt dough shapes! She has organised charity discos and raised money for the holiday home for the handicapped where she once worked. She believes that, because she is lucky enough to have all that she needs in this world materially, (which is actually not a lot!) that she should give to others less fortunate than herself, whether that be with financial help or in the giving of her time.

She believes so strongly in fairness and justice, although again she has allowed herself to be treated very badly in the past and has been unable to stand up for her own rights. She hates any kind of snobbery, and yet she continues to feel intimidated by anyone she feels inferior to, which can sadly cover an awful lot of people. I believe she would be a fantastic fighter of causes if she only had more confidence and self esteem to really believe she could make a difference.

It is this deep-rooted lack of self worth that has paralysed her over the years. She feels that everyone else is 'real' and 'grown up' but that she is such a waste of space, or that she takes up far too much space on this earth. She has so much that she wants to say, but the words cannot get past this force field of fear that is in her throat. She fears that whatever she says will sound stupid or insignificant, even though she really knows intellectually that her views are as valid as anyone else's. She has just suppressed these views for so long that she finds it difficult to articulate them, especially when confronted with people who have rather strong personalities.

She has hidden away from life as best she could for most of her days, and has only dipped her toes in the water when she has felt totally safe. Perhaps on some rare occasions she has been able to walk side by side with the fear rather than allowing it to remain the huge obstruction that it usually is. However, these times have been few and far between, and although each time becomes just a little easier, it is still a very daunting thought for her to go out into the world and live as she really wants to; as a functioning part of society-at-large. She feels safest at home—it is her only safe haven, and alone there she does not feel threatened at all, except by the ever present voices in her head.

She has days when she cannot even bring herself to walk down the street for fear of meeting someone she knows and having to talk. Those days she tends to stutter when she talks and she feels so very young and inexperienced amongst even her peers. It is as if they have all grown up as they should and she has been left behind somewhere. It is so sad because she really does want this connection with people and to feel as if she belongs—as if she is 'okay'. She has so much she wants to give to other people but she feels so empty at times that she is unable to do so.

She can be rather a manipulative person, and a controlling person, but I believe she only acts this way out of fear. If she can somehow make her world just as she wants it to be, then she can feel safe. She is not a jealous person, nor is she even envious because she feels she has all she needs materially. I think the only quality she may be slightly envious of is peace of mind, but that is all.

She is a good mother, who has always tried to do the best she can with the emotional tools she has available to her at the time. At first she tried so very hard to be the 'perfect' mother because of her own unsettled childhood but the pressure she placed upon herself was far too much. The first few years of motherhood were difficult and she will always feel guilty about those dark times. If only she could change them, she would, but she is beginning to see that she can't and that she needs to think about TODAY and not always dwell in the past. She can't always see that she is a good mother but the close relationship that she has with her daughter today is a living testament to that fact.

As for being a wife, she hasn't always known what that role entailed. Being married is a very grown up commitment, as is being a mother, so it hasn't come easy to her either. She would rather be a good partner and a friend than a 'wife' and hasn't always been able to do that because of her own very strong insecurities and fears. Because she has such low self-esteem, she is suspicious of the motives her partner has for being with her and has tested his love for her many times over the years. She has a lot to learn about adult relationships, but then her role models were very thin on the ground as she was growing up, so it is only to be expected.

She cares far less than she should about her own needs and is not even sure what they really are. She would far rather fulfil somebody else's needs than her own. She has a strong feeling that she doesn't really matter and she hasn't taken very good care of herself over the years. She was not able to ask for help for her problems until they were so bad that they were affecting the other people in her life, and she sought help as much for them as for herself. She would always reach out to help others and encourage them to seek help, but would never acknowledge her own needs or her rights to that very same help.

Now is the time that she really needs to look within herself. She needs to be warmed when she is cold, she needs to eat when she is hungry, to drink when she is thirsty and to sleep when she is tired. She needs to look after her body and not harm it as she has been doing for so many years. It is her only vehicle through this life and if she is to make the difference in this world that she truly wants to, then she must make sure that she is here to do so, fit and healthy and happy.

She needs to be able to feel the love that surrounds her and not be frightened to let it in for fear of losing it again. She needs to be able to enjoy the good times instead of being afraid of them. Good times were never the norm for her in the past and she feels so much more at home in times of trouble and fear because that is what she knows best.

She needs to feel a part of life instead of being simply a supporter on the sidelines. She needs to recognise that she has a lot to give, both to others and to herself, and she needs to learn to allow herself to do just that.

Most of all she needs to know that she is okay, and that her life is okay, and it WILL be okay, even with all its ups and owns, and that to be okay is enough…

She is a human being with both gifts and faults and that is enough too…

I am enough…

******

I cry when I read this through and I cannot believe that I have written these words about ME. I have never been so good to myself in my whole life and I have never been able to see myself for who I really am. I like this person I have written about…but is she really ME?

Am I *really* okay?

Am I *really* enough?

I am stunned and shocked and I just cannot stop crying. I feel as if, for the very first time, I have given myself permission to simply BE…

Abstinence…

It is by no means easy to 'cure' a food addiction, if such a thing even exists. There is no all or nothing solution to it—no way you can simply stop eating and cut food out of your life completely—although coming from me, that sounds rather strange! Me who attempted to do just that! But rationally, we have to eat, and so we can't avoid food in the same way that an alcoholic can stop drinking alcohol altogether, tremendously difficult though that may be.

At the OA meetings people talk about 'Abstinence' but this confuses me. How can I be abstinent? What do I have to do? How do I come to terms with having such a bad relationship with food whilst still having to eat to exist every day of my life? This is my next huge obstacle!

I have hardly ever eaten normally in my entire life. As a baby I know I was deprived of food, and then as soon as I was able to ask for more, I most certainly did. I always wanted more and more to fill that gap inside, and then I really messed things up completely when I was anorexic and bulimic. I have no idea what normal means today with regard to food. I don't know how to begin eating properly on a daily basis at all. I have to take it step by very tiny step.

Abstinence where food is concerned seemingly means cutting out the OVER-eating not the everyday eating. But first I have to discover what is normal for me to eat and what constitutes extra! God, this is hard! It must sound so strange to someone who has never had an eating disorder. After all, how can I not know what is normal for me to eat? But I really have no idea what an average portion is. I have lost all my natural instincts that tell me when I am hungry and when I have had enough to eat, as I have ridden roughshod over them for so many years. I have to start observing how much other people eat and put a similar amount on my own plate. I have to retrain my mind to accept this amount as being normal.

I always used to skip breakfast completely as I was constantly trying to be 'Good' at the start of every day. Now my Normal becomes two slices of toast and a banana, or else a small bowl of cereal. It doesn't feel at all natural to me to eat at this time of day but I have to be strict with myself and tell myself that I am at last taking care of my body's needs and be proud of myself that I am doing so. I make sure that I eat three meals a day with no food at all being on a Forbidden list. No food is 'Good' or 'Bad' any more—*I* am not 'Good' or 'Bad', I am simply a person who is trying her best these days.

I start to really listen to my body and if I do recognise a hint of hunger I respond to it as naturally as I can, with a piece of fruit or more food if it is a mealtime. If I still have food left on my plate but I feel full, I make myself stop rather than plough ahead and finish it all as I used to. It feels incredibly unnatural to leave food on a plate and very wrong when I first attempt this. I feel guilty somehow but this is my new way of being and I must follow it through.

I also ask myself questions when I crave food and am desperate to eat something—questions such as;

Do I want this food because I am physically hungry and my body needs some fuel, or am I eating for an emotional reason? Am I angry or sad or lonely or frightened? If so, then I learn to deal with the emotion rather than trying to push it back inside with food. I talk, I write it down, and I try to get it out in any way I can.

I ask myself *why* I feel this way. What has made me angry? Have I said yes when I should have said No? Do I feel resentful or bitter over something that has happened through the day? Am I asking too much of myself? I dig deeper and deeper with these questions until I find out what is *really* the matter, then I try to resolve the issue and move on. Changed days from when I ran a mile from the problem at hand and stuffed it further inside myself underneath a layer of chocolate.

Oh, it isn't as easy as it may sound—far from it. I would far rather eat during these early days than face these awful feelings and have to take the responsibility for my own life and my own actions. But I have reached a point in my existence where overeating to numb the pain is no longer an acceptable way for me to live and I have to choose an alternative path, and this is it. I am tired of hiding from the world and from myself, tired of being a scared little child who can't deal with anything remotely formidable. I need to grow up at last and there is only me who can do this for myself. Others can support me, but at the end of the day it is down to ME.

It is a very very daunting task indeed , but one which is so very worthwhile. With each day that passes I grow a little stronger and I learn a little more about this person I call Anne. I gain pride in myself for each little obstacle I overcome, for every time I am faced with the choice of chocolate or life and I choose life. For years as a child I didn't have a choice as to how I lived, and then as I grew older I didn't actually realise that I DID now have a choice. I could choose every step of the way except I had never been told I was allowed to actually participate in my own life. I perceived living as a kind of current that swept you along and you had to cope with what came at you in any way you could, good or bad. I grew up as a victim and lived as a victim for the vast majority of my life, and believe me, it is no way to live. It is a very frightening place to be—like a feather on the wind, being cast this way and that and never quite knowing where you are going to land.

I reacted to life on a daily basis and never chose my own actions in as much as I allowed other people to dictate how I would behave. But no more. I know deep down that I have a choice every second of every day now. Oh, they may not be easy choices, but they are MY choices and I take responsibility for every single one of them, whether they are good choices or less than responsible ones. They are MY choices now. I can't even begin to describe to you how incredibly empowering that feels. It makes me smile from ear to ear and all the way back again!

So I have discovered a little of my Abstinence and my Normal, and now I know how I can take care of myself. I have many days where I go right back to being the victim again and I seem to perversely enjoy those days sometimes, but at least I have something to strive for now and that means the world to me. I have goalposts, I have the beginnings of a real foundation, I have a far better relationship with food and I am on my way to becoming a far happier ME…

Paradise Lost…

I have been abstinent from compulsive overeating for months on end now, I have lost weight and I should be over the moon, but I am not. What on earth is happening to me NOW??? I seem determined to screw everything up at every turn and I am so very angry with myself. Not a very helpful reaction, I know, but it's an honest one all the same.

Today I am in Paradise—literally. There is simply no other word for it. Neil, Catherine and I have dreamed of this holiday to Florida for so long and now we are really here. We have planned what we will do, where we will go, what sights we will see, and imagined how wonderful it will be, so actually being here is a dream come true. The sun is beaming down on us, the sea is such a beautiful shimmering blue, the ocean stretches out in front of me for miles and the white sands are warm beneath my feet.

Neil and Catherine are walking along the beach collecting shells and their voices and their laughter carries on the breeze to the spot where I am sitting, staring out to sea. I am in Paradise. This moment in time is beautiful, peaceful, warm and wonderful, just perfect and just as we imagined it to be—but inside I feel so very distant from it all. I feel numb, then tense, then numb again and I am so aware that I have spent the bulk of this holiday just acting out the part of 'happy holidaymaker' rather than actually living it. Surely I haven't come all this way just to go back to pretending and playing a cameo role in my own life again?

I am on holiday, for God's sake. Most people would give anything to swap places with me and be sitting on this beach, and yet here I am feeling so incredibly miserable for no apparent reason at all. What is wrong with me? My eating is okay—in fact it is better than it has ever been—and the weight I have lost has been so natural and hasn't screwed with my head at all. Why then have I got this twisted knot in my gut again? Why do I still feel this way? What on earth is going on?

I lie in bed that night and cry quietly. I thought I had been doing so very well and was on the right track at last, but something is still holding me back. I haven't felt this low in a while now, well, not to this extent anyway. Some days I still feel down for no reason but I put it down to all that has happened in the past still surfacing so I do my best to keep going as always and try not to overeat because of it. I just don't understand what is happening to me this time.

I talk to Neil and attempt to explain to him just how I feel. I should go to the doctors when we get home, he says, but I am so against that idea. I have thought of it so many times before when I have been low like this but I know just what she would say. It's depression, she'll tell me and then she will write me a prescription for anti-depressants and I'll be out of the surgery before I know it. I really don't want to go down that road—not medication. There is no logical reason for that, or at least none other than my stupid pride again anyway. It is okay for anyone *else* to get all the help they need with their troubles but there is still that very stubborn part of me that feels **I** should somehow be able to cope without the help of medication. If I start to take pills to help me along then it is somehow not ME who has recovered; I would feel as if I were cheating in some way. No, I have to do it all on my own.

Isn't it amazing how quickly the old patterns of thinking creep back in, even when you think you have learned a better way to act and a more nurturing way to live? Why on earth do I still insist on making this so very hard for myself? Why do I still need to suffer? I am doing so very well with my eating patterns and I know that my attitudes to life are changing daily but I still have this one major hurdle that I need to climb over and deep down, I don't think that I CAN do it alone.

I know in my heart that I have suffered from depression for years—not just periods of feeling low, but a black, despairing depression that has nothing to do with what is happening externally in my life. It just IS, it exists inside me and has got so caught up with my eating disorders that I don't know where one starts and the other takes over. But now that I have found some order to my eating, the depression is staring me boldly in the face every day and I know that if I am to move any further forward I need to swallow my pride yet again and ask for help.

I really need it. I shouldn't be sitting here on a beach in Paradise wanting to sob my heart out, should I? I need to ask for help…

******

Two weeks after we arrive home from our holiday I am sitting in front of my doctor saying the words I have rehearsed so many times, over and over in my head.

"This is so difficult for me to talk about," I begin and the doctor puts down her pen and prescription pad and sits back to listen. "I have been feeling so very low for so long now and I just can't seem to cope any more."

The doctor is wonderful and I couldn't have asked for a more sympathetic and understanding response to my plea for help. She smiles at me, talks to me, listens to me, spends time reassuring me that what I am feeling is by no means crazy or unusual in our high-pressured world. It has a real name, this condition.

Clinical Depression.

I have Clinical Depression. An imbalance of the chemicals in certain areas of my brain. And yes, she can give me medication to help. Nothing addictive, though, she promises me, and nothing too strong. No way do I want to sleep my way through my days or feel so detached from myself that I can't function as ME, as I have seen happen to some people on antidepressants. The doctor also says she will request a period of psychotherapy for me so that I can talk over any issues that may be contributing to the depression. Talking helps a lot, she tells me. Don't I know it?! A combination of medication and psychotherapy should help me greatly and I can also go back to talk to her any time I need to. Plus, I am to have monthly checkups with her anyway to see how I am coping with it all. I will be fine, she tells me, and I just need a little help along the way.

I walk out of that surgery with a prescription for Prozac in my hand and such a feeling of relief that I have actually told the doctor what is happening in my life and have been taken seriously for once by a professional. I still have very mixed feelings about taking these pills—one half of me is logical and says that if my brain chemicals are imbalanced, then what is wrong with taking one small pill a day to help put them right? But the old perfectionist side of me feels as if I have failed. I should have been able to cope on my own. I should never have asked anyone for help.

It takes me quite a while to reconcile these two differing opinions which exist within me, but for the time being I choose to follow the logical side of me which I trust more and more these days and I take the Prozac every day. I am learning even more to take care of myself, however tough that may be at times…

My Dull, Grey Place

I am in a dull, grey place today,
With a heavy heart
And clumsy hands,
So full of doubts and fears.
But I tell myself
This is just a temporary stopping place
And to look to the skies
With the knowledge inside
That tomorrow all may be well,

It didn't used to be this way.
My dull, grey place was once
A dark, black prison.
My bars were fears that never left me,
My only comfort, food.
I lived a life of shame and not belonging,

Of a happy face but a dying soul,
A life of no way out,
Or so I thought…

And so I sit in this dull, grey place
And think, "Well, maybe it's not so bad—
My fears aren't bars,
And the comfort comes from deep within
And not from a fridge today.
For that I'm eternally grateful
And I look forward to the light…

******

Three months later it is Christmas Day and I can honestly say that this is the first Christmas for years that I have actually felt a real part of the celebrations happening around me. So many times in the past I have felt as if I were merely going through the motions and acting as I thought I *should* act just to fit in and be 'normal'. I was always being what other people expected me to be, and not really existing in that moment as a person within my own right. Either that or feeling guilty or sad about something in my past, or dreading having to face some event in the future. Living in the moment had never really been an option for me before.

But since taking the Prozac it feels as if a murky veil has been lifted from in front of my eyes and I can see, and hear, and touch and smell and feel – *really* feel for the first time ever. Oh, I have always been able to feel the negative, terrifying feelings, but warm and joyful times always eluded me, but now…ah, now I can even feel *them* too.

I sit today watching Catherine open her Christmas presents and I am HAPPY. My God, I am HAPPY!!!!!!! I even do a spot check and search around the corners of my mind for any remnants of fear or anger which may be lurking there, ready to rear their ugly heads, but there are none. Not even a tiny one. Right this very minute in time, here and now, I am happy and oh, it feels so GOOD!!!!!!

Even better is the fact that I have had no side effects at all from taking the Prozac. It doesn't make me sleepy; it doesn't make me hyper. I don't see any difference in me physically in that I have no new aches and pains. No, what this medication makes me feel is OKAY. I feel alive. I feel I can reach out and touch the world and be a part of it without being held back by the manic voices, or without my fingers coming up against this protective curtain of fear that always came between me and real life.

Of course the medication is not a panacea for all ills and I have my down days as well, but they are so much easier to accept these days. This is normal. This is part of life. I am NEVER going to encounter a time where I am happy every single minute of every day. Life is never going to be perfect—although it has taken me long enough to reconcile myself to that fact! No, the Prozac is just another valuable tool in my life that helps me become all that I can be. It frees a part of my mind to help me in my quest to live as well as I can. It isn't magic, it most certainly doesn't do any of the hard groundwork for me and I still have a lot to work on emotionally and a lot of my past to come to terms with, but it is a tool, and at last I am eager to accept all the help I can get.

Today, I am sitting in my own home, with my husband and my daughter, and I am safe and warm. I will eat far too much, just as everyone else does at Christmas and I will feel full but I won't feel 'Bad' today for being that way. I will relax and watch all the old repeats on TV, moan at the mountain of washing up in the kitchen and watch Catherine play with her new toys. I feel such a sense of joy flow through me today and I will know that I am exactly where I am meant to be at this very moment in time.

Now THIS is Paradise…

Today is a Good Day…

Yes…I am very happy to report, with my hand on my heart, that today IS a good day, and although it sounds so very simple, it is little short of a miracle to me. Not too long ago I would find it amazing to think I could even have a good *minute*, never mind a whole day of them! I almost don't want to say that my day is good just in case I jinx it somehow and there's actually a whole skip-load of crap just waiting for me around the corner! But, today IS a good day and I feel brave, so I've gone ahead and said it anyway—(but if I don't happen to finish this piece of writing, you'll know that the skip-load got me after all!)

So what constitutes this good day of mine? A win on the lottery? A new job? Inheriting thousands of pounds from an old Aunty I didn't even know I had? No…not even close… Today is such a good day for the simple reason that I feel just fine. I'm okay….I'm okay, and that is really all I've ever wanted to be.

I got out of bed today and waited for my heart and my head to give me at least a hint as to what was in store for me today. If the minute I open my eyes, my brain switches on to fast forward and has already told me a dozen things to be scared of before I've even sat up in bed, then I know I'm in for a rough time. If the minute I awake, my heart feels as if it is wrapped up tightly in an old wet towel and my stomach is churning around like a full washing machine, then I know I won't be dancing my way through breakfast. And by lunchtime I will likely be biting the heads off small animals! (Only joking!)

On those kinds of days I have to take a really deep breath, force myself upright and keep reminding myself to go gently through this day, for it will most probably not be any easy one. And that is a great understatement for the many days I have endured over the past years due to my bouts of depression. Other days see me marginally less frantic and I am able to curtail my urge to maim small creatures until at least evening, but even those days can be tough to get through with any degree of sanity. Just ask my family!

However, I never gave up the hope that one of these days I would wake up just feeling ...OKAY! I wasn't aiming for the stars; I didn't want to be deliriously happy' or full of the joys of spring' or the life and soul of even my *own* party. No, I just wanted to feel okay. To be able to sit contentedly with myself, to have some peace in my head and my heart and to know that I was okay, that I was enough and that I counted for something.

I can't get over quite how simple that all sounds and I suppose that to the majority of people it IS simple. They just get up and go about their days, with the usual moans about the weather and a laugh here and there with their friends or colleagues, and they never seem to give a second thought to their state of mind. They don't have to pluck up the courage to pick up the phone when all they want to do is dial the speaking clock. They don't sit rigid on the sofa, trying to weigh up whether they have the bottle to go across the road to the supermarket, and I'm sure they don't live in fear of having to actually pass the time of day with another human being.

Not that I'm saying that life is a bed of roses for those who don't suffer from depression. I know that the world has plenty of skip-loads of that aforementioned crap and that it gets pelted around a fair bit. But depression has that awkward twist that makes people afraid of every last thing in the world for no logical reason at all, and, top of the list, I was terrified of myself.

I say 'was', which makes it sound as if I will never be that way again, but I know that one good day doesn't make a summer (or should that be 'swallow?'). Whatever, I am not blasé enough about my condition that I think I am 'cured' because I have one day where I can actually smile and the effort doesn't crack my jaw! But instead I feel truly grateful for this whole, complete good day in my life. I feel as if I want to hang on to it or at least frame it somehow and put it on my wall to remind myself on those bad days that I CAN actually do it! I feel as if I've just run my first four minute mile, and even though I may not be able to do it again tomorrow or even the next day, I have the knowledge deep inside that I *am* capable of it and that is what counts the most.

Yes, today is indeed a good day. I talked to a lady at the bus stop and I didn't once feel as if I'd said something totally ridiculous or, indeed, that I had no right to be having this conversation at all. I didn't even stutter and I managed to look her in the eye as well. It's far better than gazing down at my left shoe as I usually do!

I was able to eat an ordinary lunch today and then stop right there, without wanting to eat the rest of the contents of the biscuit tin, the fridge, and my daughter's supply of sweets from Granny. I didn't need even a chocolate digestive to feel better about myself today—I was able to do that all on my own!

I took on all the household chores that I really HAD to do, without feeling so under pressure from every last job on my list. On a bad day I can sit down and weep if I have to so much as wash up the breakfast dishes, and if it's the cat's litter tray that needs cleaning…well, you might as well just put me out of my misery there and then, it's so bad!

I realise I make light of it all here, but I know from much personal experience that these bad days are torture and that if I didn't have a tiny piece of humour left lurking somewhere inside me, I would never have come through it this far at all. The very last way to describe depression is humorous, and the words have not yet been invented to aptly portray the seemingly endless despair that accompanies it, nor the physical pain deep down inside, made up of so many twisted and distorted feelings that have never been allowed out.

On a bad day I want to shrink away from life and I yearn to be so teeny tiny that no one can see me at all. I want to curl up under the covers and sink into unconsciousness so that I do not have to greet the day or the multitude of challenges it brings. I feel as if I don't deserve to take up even the smallest space on this earth, and I disgust myself by taking up probably twice the space that I should (which is due to those sweet sugary remedies I feed myself when the pain is too much).

But today…ah, today I can fill my space in this world deliciously and feel as if I have an absolute right to do so. I have a right to walk down the High Street and into a shop and to buy something and I don't for once think that everyone is staring at me or that they can see into my head and know the madness that sometimes dwells there.

Today there is enough peace inside my head for me to complete my sentences without forgetting the most simple of words. I can even write out a shopping list! And speak coherently when I phone a friend. Heavens!!…I can even phone a friend! It is amazing! The simple joys in life…today they are mine…all mine…

And tomorrow…well, who knows? Not me for sure, and today I don't think I really need to know either. For even if I wake up tomorrow with the demons back in residence in my brain and the fear firmly lodged in my heart, at least I will have had this day. I will have the memory of this day to carry with me as ammunition- to show that it is really possible and I can be okay for a whole, perfect, wonderful day…

Yes, today was, indeed, a good day…Thank you so very much….

Chapter Six

A Slice of Gateau for the Lady!

Food

Food equals Love, Warmth, Comfort and Safety.
Most of us learn that as soon as we utter our first cries upon this Earth,
But some of us also learn that Hunger equals No Love at all, Isolation, Cold and Fear,
And we learn that far too soon,
And it becomes embedded deep in our souls.

As we grow up, Food and Hunger become tools that we use to punish ourselves.
We feel Unloved, Unworthy, so we deprive ourselves of Food.
Or else we crave Love and Warmth and Safety so much that we gorge ourselves with Food.
This strange distortion of Self is echoed by the way we fail to nurture our bodies.
To be Empty equals being Pure and Clean.
To be Full equals being Disgusting, out of Control, and Bad,
We never find the security we need in the Food, not for long anyway.
And so it goes on…

One day when we are ready, we can let go of this powerful emotional crutch of ours.
Not all at once, but bit by bit in tiny teeny steps
As we learn to trust ourselves and build our own foundations.
We give to ourselves the Love and Acceptance we should have been nurtured with long ago.
We feed our souls, we waken our spirits.
We give ourselves permission to BE, to take up our rightful place on this Earth

And to become the best that we can be with the tools that we have.

And so today, for me, and for many others, Food equals a way to stay alive
And Love, Warmth, Comfort and Safety come from deep within,
No longer from a chocolate bar, but from my very soul…

So What of Today?…

Today my life is almost unrecognisable from the one I lived even five years ago. I am not a different person as such, but I have finally allowed myself to grow into the person I was meant to be; the person beneath the little girl who was always hiding and afraid to come out just in case she got hurt. The person who was so afraid to BE that she constantly tried to destroy herself for fear of being found out. Today I don't live in the shadows any more. Oh, I might run back in there sometimes when the going gets tough, but it is only a temporary stopping place now, and not a place to permanently spend my days.

My life today is full of little achievements every single day. Little to the outside world at least, but huge to me and to anyone else who has an understanding of someone who has lived through an eating disorder and depression. My achievements today will never be recognised by certificates or promotion or medals but they register deep inside me and fill me with immense pride. I want to share them with the world, not just so that I can get a pat on the back—although that is lovely too! But because I so want to shout out that if it can happen for me, then it can happen for you as well. I am nobody special, no more special than anyone else in this world. I have no unique talents, I am not superhuman, I am an ordinary human being and what I can do, then so can you and much more too.

Take heart from my Todays…they can be your Todays as well. They WILL be your Todays.

Believe me.

******

Today I am able to walk into a supermarket, buy as many bars of chocolate as I wish, and know for sure that they are not all going to end up in my stomach that very same day! Twenty years down the line, I really *am* buying them for the family and it gives me such a sense of pride and achievement that I have come such a long way since those awful 'selection box' days.

I want to shout out to the woman at the checkout and the customers in the queue behind me and to the people on the bus on the way home, "Look at me! Look at all the chocolate I can buy now and it's really *not* all for me!" But I generally manage to retain a shred of sanity and just content myself with an inner glow instead!

For I *know* now that I won't rip off the wrappers as soon as I get home and wolf down the contents all in one go. More than likely I will leave them sitting there in the carrier bag in the hall until I have tripped over them enough times to warrant moving them at last and that is a world away from how it used to be. It is a truly amazing feeling for someone who couldn't even have one chocolate biscuit in the house for many years for fear of it triggering a binge that could last for days.

I have a huge biscuit box at home, an old bread bin in fact, which I fill up with the chocolate bars when I get in and there they stay. I put them away and then I simply carry on with my day. The chocolate doesn't haunt my every waking moment as it used to. In fact, I barely even think of it at all, only when we are all having some chocolate together and then my only problem is to decide which ONE bar to have! Which ONE!!!!!!!!! Not TEN or TWENTY. I can stop at ONE today and it is enough and my mind isn't pulled back to the box like a magnet, with every inch of my being craving more. At last I am (almost!) normal!

For most people I know that this is an everyday occurrence but for me this is a true gift. To be free of the shackles of a food addiction, and an eating disorder...oh, it is a joy that I have no real words for…it is Heaven on earth…

******

Today I can wake up in the morning very slowly and calmly– unless the rotten alarm clock is set, of course!—and gradually I become aware of the world around me. The radio beside my bed is always on so my mind unconsciously sings along with whatever song is playing as I awake. Maybe I can hear the birds singing outside my window, or the rain falling onto the road outside, or the cat purring on the bed beside me. I register this new day and wake up slowly and peacefully.

My first thoughts can be about anything in the world today. What day is it? What do we have planned? Can I lie here a little longer? Is it sunny? What did I dream about last night?

Gone are the days when the minute I woke up I was bombarded with an interrogation from the ever-present voices in my head...The Food Squad!

What did I eat last night? Was I Good or Bad? Can I eat today? How much am I allowed? Did I leave anything over after my binge last night? God, I *must* get up and exercise...NOW!

Instantly I would be in panic mode back then, on red alert, ready and waiting for the minute I would be faced with temptation and ready to fight it at all times, successfully or otherwise. There was no lying there snug and warm in my bed, revelling in the cosiness and comfort, and looking forward to a brand-new day. Instead it was mental torture from the minute I awoke until the minute I fell asleep again a whole day later.

But today I am mostly free of all that. Oh yes, I have days when I wake up slightly less than full of the joys of Spring, but that just makes me human, doesn't it? No, what means the most to me today is that my mind doesn't automatically spring to the subject of food the minute I surface. Today food is sometimes way down on my list of first thoughts—so far down in fact that occasionally I even forget to have breakfast! Not very often though—I can never see myself being the kind of person who forgets to eat very often!

Ah, I just love the fact that today I can wake up in peace and greet the day with a smile.

******

Today I can relax.

Absolutely and completely.

Today I can walk along the beach and listen to the waves splashing on the shore, feel the sun on my face, and experience such a connection to the world that I am so energised by this positive attack on my senses. My mind can be still, or else I can drift off and daydream. REAL daydreams as well—not what should I have for tea or will I fit into that dress for tonight, or how much more do I need to walk along this beach before I have used up the calories in the small apple I ate by mistake? No, it is nothing like that today.

I walk when I want, I sit when I want, lie down when I want, which again I know is quite normal for most people. But I was always so wrapped up in the amount of calories going in and out of my body that every movement I made, every position I was in equalled a number. If I ate more than I should, then I had to move more or I wasn't allowed to sit down until I was sure all the extra calories had gone from my system. It is a totally manic way to live. Totally unnatural and mind-blowing. It means you can never be at peace inside your own mind. You can never relax enough just in case you are caught off guard and a few extra calories sneak their way in here or there like that one apple did all those years ago, and many times since. What a sad way to live…but at the time it was all I had. All that I knew was possible for me.

Today I don't have to live that way, thank goodness. I don't count calories anymore (well, only if my life spins wildly out of control again and I need an old familiar coping strategy to cling on to, but that's not too often, thank goodness). I don't measure my energy expenditure at all, and many days I am downright lazy! I can watch TV and really see what is happening in front of my eyes, or read a book and be really engrossed in it, instead of my brain always half-listening to one of the many self-destruct tapes that seemed to run constantly in my head.

Today my mind can be still. Heavens, I have even been to meditation classes and found that I can almost still it completely! Peace of mind—what a wonderful but quite elusive quality that is. I don't have it all the time, of course…who does? But I have it at least *some* of *most* days and that is far better than the NEVER that it used to be…

******

Today I have boundaries of my very own. Today I can say 'No' if I mean it and 'Yes' if I want to. I don't have to do everything to please the people around me anymore or *be* everything to everyone. I won't allow myself to be treated badly today—well, not more than once anyway. I have more than an ounce of self-respect for myself now, and most of the time I believe I deserve to take up my space on the Earth. I know that phrase comes up a lot in my writings but when you live your life apologising all the time for even *being*, it is amazing when you feel at last that it is okay for you to simply exist.

I have developed real principles, morals and values that are all mine, and not merely adopted from somebody else's way of living. I have a very strong view of right and wrong, I know what I want to do with each day that arrives. I have definite goals in life, I see a real future for myself –a GOOD future—whereas once I couldn't even see beyond the blackness of the day.

I want to *live* today. And I appreciate every new day of life that I am given, because for years I hated every day that dawned and didn't want to be part of another single one. I wanted so badly to simply disappear, to die, to not exist anymore, and life became a dizzy merry go round of pain and fear. But now

I am so very grateful for the times when I just stared at the bottle of pills and then put them away again unopened. What I would have missed in my life if I had ended it all back then. What joys I would never have known. I am eternally grateful that, however bad it became for me over the years, there was always this small spark inside me which kept me struggling on. It's the survival instinct, I suppose, but thank goodness I had it in abundance when I needed it.

That spark has grown into a really powerful life force today and it has allowed me to begin to create the person I always knew deep down I was supposed to be. Today I can be ME and I simply don't have to apologise to anyone for that.

And if you're still out there, Emma…

Nonentity?? Me??

You must be joking…

******

Today I realise that I DO have a choice in my life. I always have a choice. I always have done, except that I could never see it. I played the role of victim for so long, and believe it or not, it is actually an easier role to play in life. Not a happy role by any means, but it avoids having to make decisions and taking responsibility for your own path through life and when you make mistakes it is far easier to blame someone else than to look to yourself for solutions.

I have been a victim for most of my life because I had never been taught any other way to live. We do as we see, and I saw people all around me who bemoaned their lot in life, or in my Nanna's case, she just accepted what she was given and got on and lived it. It took me many years to realise that I had a choice in the matter and that I didn't have to be swept along with the tide of life. I could stand up and say 'No' and turn in the opposite direction if I felt I was heading the wrong way. I wish I had had that knowledge back then, but I do today and that is what counts the most.

And how incredibly empowering it is to take back your own strength instead of forever giving it away to other people. To have faith in your own capabilities and to know that whatever comes along you will deal with it and you will be okay. To live without the terror of what is hiding round the next corner. To feel that you *can* cope, that you can *really* cope and you're not just putting on that brave face anymore. What an amazing revelation that is! A real life-changing revelation.

However, it doesn't happen overnight, and like all the most precious things in life, you have to keep working at it. I'm never going to be one of these people who just seem to sail through life and have an inner serenity all the time (if indeed they really exist anyway!). No, I have to work at it every day to some extent and keep reminding myself that I am okay and that all will be well. Some days I am more successful than others, but I am very rarely a victim these days.

I *always* have a choice as to how I react to any given situation and I try to make sure I remember that incredibly important fact. Nobody actually *makes* us do anything—we choose to act in a certain way because we much prefer to do that than to deal with the consequences of doing just the opposite. But I never felt as if I could choose anything at all in my life, and it was almost as if it was all predetermined for me and all I could do was follow my allotted footsteps. But I know now that ultimately I can choose every last move that I make on this earth and that is still incredible to me.

Do I overeat tonight to dull the pain or do I fight the fear instead? It is my choice…

Do I baby-sit for a friend even though I am shattered and I really want an early night? Or do I risk disappointing her and saying 'No? Again, it is my choice…

Do I get upset because I feel rejected or abandoned or do I look rationally at the situation and see what is really behind it all? It is my choice…

It is *always* my choice.

We really do have far more power than we have ever realised, and when we tap into that power, it gives us such an immense surge of freedom and pride. It doesn't take much searching to find your own power either—you just need someone to tell you that you have it and that you have a perfect right to own it. Just accept that it is there, keep reminding yourself that you can choose your own way and just see what wonderful things happen to you…just see…you will be truly amazed.

******

Today I have *real* friends; friends who will stand by me through thick and thin (excuse my poor choice of words there!), who will never judge me, and who will share their lives with me. They can share their hopes and their dreams, and allow me the wonderful gift of doing exactly the same with them.

I have never been particularly successful with friendships throughout my life, being the 'fat girl' who hung round the fringes of a crowd and was never one of the 'chosen few'. I always believed that I had to give and give even more to people and always be there for them, regardless of whether or not they afforded me the same luxury. Consequently I was a sitting target for anyone seeking a doormat as a friend—me with 'Walk all over me' tattooed in bold print upon my forehead!

I often allowed myself to be treated badly, unfairly, insensitively, even cruelly, and I could never bring myself to utter a word in my defence for fear of losing that particular 'friend'. After all, any friend was better than no friend at all in my eyes. And when that is the standard you set for yourself, then those kinds of friends are precisely what you will find.

I am not saying that I have never had good friends until today, but they were nothing like the balanced, open and honest friendships that I have in my life now. There was always this vulnerable side of me that I felt I just *had* to keep to myself, even with the closest of friends. I could never admit to them that I was scared or lonely or angry or in the least bit needful. No, I always had to appear to be coping, even when my life was falling apart around my ears. I couldn't even ask my best friends for help. I still had to keep that smile rigidly fixed to my face and pretend I was basically okay. Many of the friends I have had in the past had no idea at all that I had eating disorders and depression and they looked at me aghast if I ever managed plucked up the courage to tell them about it later on. 'But we never realised…you always looked so happy…' Bring on the Oscars again!

But today I am able to open up my heart and allow people to see who I am really am, warts and all. I take the risks that would have driven me to a major binge in the past. I say what I feel. If I am sad, I can share it. If I am angry, I can explain why. It is no shame for me to be seen as less than perfect now because I never was anyway, and nobody ever can be. But I didn't realise that myself for a long long time and nobody ever told me otherwise. I couldn't let anyone apart from Neil and Catherine see me at anything other than my best, and before I went to OA I would rather have died than have uttered the words 'I am having a bad time'. I denied so much of myself, even hated big chunks of who I was, and if *I* didn't like me, then how on earth could I expect anyone else to?

But, do you know what? Even the negative aspects of my character sit fairly well with me today because I have finally learned that we are all made up of a whole array of emotions, some of them good and some of them not so good. It is all part of being human and at last I have accepted that to be human, with all the flaws that it entails, is just what I am meant to be. Today everything is okay, and what's more, *I* am okay. I quite like Me in fact, so it is okay for others to like me as well…finally!

And when I finally accepted that I am a decent human being, some wonderful people appeared in my life as if by magic. People who care, who listen, who share their stories with me, and who are always there for me. People I can give to, love and care for, and who enrich my life beyond anything I could ever have hoped for. They are my friends, my new family, and my soul mates…

To those people who know they have a lifelong place in my heart, a very big Thank You from me to you…You know who you are…

******

Today I am a mother and a pretty good one at that, even though I do say so myself! I always wanted to be a good mother—no, that's not exactly true—I always wanted to be a *Perfect* mother, which is a whole other thing altogether, and a pretty fruitless desire at that. It took me several rocky years of striving to be perfect with Catherine before I was able to let go enough to be as good a mother as I can be on any given day with the tools I have at my disposal.

I remember my own childhood as being so very fraught, so frantic, so traumatic, and also so silent. Nobody seemed to talk to me and explain what was happening in my world, and I grew up desperate for communication, desperate to understand the people in my life and with a great need to be heard. I am quite a communication junkie now!

But I was determined that it was never going to be like that for Catherine. Never was she going to lie awake at night, terrified of what the next day would bring, scared stiff of what might be hiding in the shadows and frightened even to go next door into her parents room to be told everything is okay for fear of being told off. Consequently we have the most open relationship I have ever had with another human being and it is still incredible to me to think that I am one half of this amazing friendship.

We can talk about absolutely anything and do, for hours! It is almost as if we are growing up together as I live, *really* live through the years that I missed in my childhood and early teens. Oh, I am not living *through* her as I know so well that she is an individual with her own life and her own needs, but I am right here living *beside* her and doing my very own growing up too. We learn together. We face situations together, figure out the best way through them and move on. We clear up each problem as it comes up, we don't just push them aside and pretend they never existed. It is a real revelation to me that we can live this way and it fills me with such a sense of pride to know that, with the help of this lovely person who is my daughter, we have turned the past around and made something incredible rise up out of the ashes.

Never will there be any secrets in our little family—none other than Christmas and birthday presents anyway! Catherine knows about my eating disorders and my depression, even more so since she has been reading the chapters of this book as I have been writing them. She has lived through thirteen years of my ups and downs, seen me in floods of tears and the depths of despair, and also as high as a kite and living my life as if each minute were the last. Oh, and everything else in-between, of course!

And one of the most important things I have been able to teach her along the way was that, whatever was happening to me was *not her fault.* I can remember one of the girls at OA telling me that she grew up feeling that every inch of sadness and anger that came out of her mother was *her* fault because nobody ever told her otherwise. I remembered all the guilt that I carried with me from the times when I took on board the blame for the bad situations in my childhood, and I made sure that every time things went wrong for me, Catherine knew it was down to ME and never her. No way is she going to grow up shouldering *my* burden as well. She has to be free to grow without the shackles of my past holding her back as they did to me for so many years.

I know she has seen a lot in her life that children shouldn't see really. Depression is an awful illness and it makes people suffer in ways that can only be imagined by those who have never fallen prey to it. I wish it had been different and that I had been one of those mothers who baked apple pies with a beaming smile on her face and always had everything under control, except that I am beginning to think they only exist in movies anyway! But I wasn't. I was and I am ME. And I do believe that seeing me accept the way I am and seeing me trying to dig my way out of my vat of grey soup has given Catherine the knowledge that she can be less than perfect too. She can grow up knowing that it is okay to be angry or sad or whatever you may feel as long as you make something good come out of it after you have had a damned good wallow!

Life's lessons aren't always the way we would envisage them, and I like to think now that I have been the best mother I could be at any given time. As the years go by I am a better mother for sure, and a very good friend to this beautiful soul who has chosen to share my life, as she is to me. And what fun we have too! We laugh until we cry, we dance, we sing, we walk along walls, we go away together and have adventures, we explore the world together—every little nook and cranny—and we really *live.* We appreciate it all, every little thing on this earth, and most of all, we love and appreciate each other. How blessed I am to have her in my life.

And just as proof of the fact that she really DOES like me too, here are some wonderful words she presented me with on my fortieth birthday. They touched my soul in a way that no words have ever done before. I am amazed that she can see the ME that it took me so very long to find…(although I dispute a few of the compliments!! Amazing cook?? Me??)

My Mum is…
by Catherine.

Always there for you
Great to talk to
Very clever
An amazing cook
A person who has a memory that goes on forever
Incredibly beautiful
Funny
Very good at writing stories
Very good at painting
Very good at playing the keyboard
Always supportive
A cup of tea making genius
A person with good taste in everything
Great at buying presents
Very organised
A wonderful teacher
A very good artist
A person very good at solving problems
Very good at remembering to feed the pets
Not afraid to be different
Very fun to be with
Charitable
Friendly
Very honest, in a good way

Always responsible
Creative
Always interesting to chat to
Understanding
A very good singer
Inventive
A song writing genius
Reliable
Always early
A star
But most of all, my Mum is...GREAT!!!

****

Just think, once upon a time I thought that I had messed my body up so much that I would never be able to have children at all. Once upon a time I thought I would never dare be intimate enough with anyone to actually conceive a child. And once upon a time I believed I would make a terrible mother because of all the traumas of my own childhood.

But I got it slightly wrong, didn't I?

I am a mother.

Not a perfect mother, but I am the best I can be.

And reading that testament to the Mum I have become makes my heart soar...

If I do nothing else in my life, I have broken the chain, I have turned the tables and made life okay for another human being, and for one whom I love with every fibre of my being...

Thank you, Catherine, for helping me grow, and allowing me to do the same for you...you are indeed a wonderful gift...

A Letter for Catherine
And for the little girl in me....

To my very special girl, Catherine,

If I could make your whole life free of fear and pain, then I would for sure. If I could make it so that you never had any doubts or worries or fears, then I would in an instant. But I have learned over the years that life is a complex fabric, woven with shiny golden cotton, dark jet-black threads and many shades in-between. Nobody has a perfect life in this world, however much it may appear that they do. We all suffer, we all experience joy, we are all a mish mash of emotions in one beautiful shell.

I have begun to see human life as one long chain; we live our life as best we can, thrive in our happiness, wander through our mistakes and mourn our sorrows. We hopefully pass on our knowledge and our wisdom to our children, who in turn carry on this chain of life lessons and add a little more along the way. Each generation can then improve the quality of life for the next...or at least I think that is how it is supposed to work!

So what can I pass on to you? What have I learned from my chequered past? What can you take from me to improve your life and build upon to pass on to your own children? I'm not arrogant enough to think that I have all the answers—I wish! Life would have been a whole lot simpler if I had! But maybe you can glean a little knowledge from the path I have walked that will make your journey through life a little easier. That is all that I wish for...Now let me see what I can find for you...

Always be true to yourself. Listen to that still, small voice deep inside that tells you which way to go next. That is your gut feeling, your soul, your intuition—call it what you will. If you feel uncomfortable with any situation you encounter, then take a step back from it if you can and give yourself a moment to think it through before you commit yourself either way. Too many times I have just jumped right in with my eyes closed, simply because I have felt pressured into giving an answer that I wasn't yet ready for. Take a deep breath, and always follow your heart.

Taking care of yourself is NOT selfish! It is self-CARE, and it should be the number one priority in your life. If you are a strong, happy and healthy individual, then you can do a huge amount of good in this world and really make a difference to the people you meet. But if you take care of others first and foremost and forget to look after yourself in the process, then you will soon be operating as an empty shell. I lived like that for so many years. I was always giving out to others just so that I would have their love and approval, but along the way I totally forgot to look after myself and then I looked to other people to fill me up, or worse still, to food addictions to make me feel whole. I failed miserably at every turn and ended up resenting the very people I was giving to in my life because I so badly wanted what they had. Believe me, there isn't a single thing anyone else in this world can do to make you feel like a whole human being; that is down to YOU alone. Make sure that you do just that. Top up your own emotional fuel on a regular basis, before attempting to go out and do the same for somebody else. None of us can operate on Empty for very long before something gives inside.

Don't ever feel that you have to follow the crowd unless you are sure, in your heart of hearts that this is the crowd you really want to be in! Accept that we are all different, we are all unique, despite the uniforms that some people choose to wear and whatever groups we may belong to along the way. You are a very special person and you are here on this Earth for your own purposes. Live your life YOUR way, not as somebody else would have you live it. Respect others along the way and honour their differences too, but always be strong enough to be who you are meant to be.

Don't compare yourself to others if you can at all help it. And don't be fooled into thinking that just because you don't look like the models on the catwalk, that you are somehow not acceptable. That is just trash. Fashions change from generation to generation, based on the fads of someone in an office somewhere who probably has the biggest inferiority complex of all! It is all just a sham, a façade. You will never be thin enough, or tall enough, or blonde enough, or rich enough, or 'whatever' enough, no matter how hard you try, because these are all external ways of feeling good about who you are. And if you don't feel good on the inside, then no amount of changing your appearance is going to make you feel happier in yourself. If it worked that way, then why would so many beautiful models, pop singers and film stars need to go into rehab so often? Wouldn't they all be deliriously happy? Underneath this shell we are all the same, so don't be fooled into thinking that appearances matter above all else. Be happy being what you are, wear what you like, do what you really enjoy doing. Be YOU. Nobody else can be!

Fill your life with positive thoughts and positive people wherever possible. Negativity drains you immensely, and makes you feel lethargic and hopeless, frustrated and resentful. It puts you in a place with no windows and no light. It turns you into a victim and makes you completely dependable on the people around you to make you feel better. Empower yourself with positive thoughts, smile, and try to see the best in life and in other people. You always have a choice in the matter, whether it feels that way or not. It really is a case of the glass being half empty or half full, however clichéd that may seem. Of course, some days are just going to be half empty days, no matter how hard we try, and those are the days when we just draw the curtains and take very good care of ourselves until we come through it. But most days we can fight the demons and just flow with positive energy. Don't swim in the grey soup of negativity without having at least one good life jacket at hand! Music, books, a good film, a long bubble bath, a walk, do whatever you can do to make yourself smile again...

Try not to think of your problems as insurmountable. There is always an answer, maybe just not an instant one! Relax, write down your thoughts and feelings if needs be, but never let any situation in this world overwhelm you so much that you can't deal with it on whatever basis you are able to. And never be too proud to ask for help. There is always someone out there who has been where you are and will be all too willing to pass on their wisdom to you. That is what we human beings do best! Reach out to someone who has walked your walk and you will find an abundance of strength and support out there.

Never, EVER, give up! This is the most important lesson of all because it keeps us alive. Look at me! Look at what I went through and then think of the mother that you have in your life today who can sometimes laugh so much that she even throws up! Think of the many dark corners I have inhabited in my life and then think of me singing like a maniac and embarrassing the hell out of you! If ***I*** *can know such fear and pain, and then find the kind of joy which fills my whole being from head to toe, then it is possible for anyone to do just the same. There is always a way past any obstacle. When a situation looks hopeless, it is only because we haven't found the right angle to view it from. There is always a way out...*

Catherine, I love you with my heart and soul, and with all of my being, more than I ever thought it was possible for me to love anyone. I know I wasn't there for you emotionally as I wanted to be at the start of your life, but I hope you can now understand why, and I hope more than anything that I have made up for it many times over in the years that have followed.

Thank you for the incredible bond that we now share, the deep friendship we have, the honesty, the openness, the fun times we have together, the way we know what the other is thinking and our ability to say whatever we feel without fear of being ridiculed. There are no secrets in our life (well, I'm sure you have some, being a teenager, but that's not the kind of stuff that I mean!). There is nothing between us that we have to keep hidden, nothing that we can never talk about. For years I was locked in a prison of shameful secrets and the honesty that I can share with you today is a real miracle to me, and one that I will never ever take for granted.

If there is one thing I can be eternally grateful for, it is that you are part of my life today. And that my life is totally unrecognisable from the one portrayed through most of this book. (Okay, that's two!) I am proud to be ME today, and more than proud to be your mother and your friend.

Go out into the world on your own terms, Catherine. Be YOU, be all that you ARE and never ever forget that you are ALWAYS enough...

Much love forever,
Mum. XXXXXXXXX

One Slice or Two?...

I don't know how many times I have snuck up to my room at Nanna's, or closeted myself in my bedroom here at home and eaten my way through an entire gateau. Not a huge one...well, not often anyway! But still one large enough to feed a fair few people and not just meant for one person. There is something so very comforting about sitting with a whole cake in front of you and working your way through it all spoonful by spoonful, and knowing all the while that it is yours, all yours...

I could never have had just one slice of gateau and then put the rest away in the fridge for later. Never. That cake would have talked out loud to me as surely as if it were alive and would have tempted me back for the rest of it in minutes. Back then I infinitely preferred overeating to the fears and the deep sense of loss that I felt if I had said No and left the cake where it was, and I yearned and ached for the comfort and safety that the food gave me, however fleetingly.

Today I haven't eaten an entire gateau to myself for longer than I can remember. Not that I don't ever get the urge to do so, but it is those urges that are fleeting now and not the momentary fix I used to get from the excess food. I don't know when I last ate a whole box of chocolates to myself, or ten chocolate bars or a whole packet of biscuits...and that feels, oh, so good.

Also I am able to actually share my precious food with others now, which I never could before. It used to be that if I bought or was given a box of chocolates, then I had to eat every last one of them myself or else the whole experience would be somehow marred. It felt as if I was giving away actual pieces of myself if I so much as gave away one chocolate or a bite of my cake. I couldn't allow anyone else into my binges. They were MINE. Many times it felt as if they were all I had left in the world that was mine, which sounds rather dramatic, I know, but that is just how it was. When your life is turned upside down on a regular basis, there is very little that you can control apart from your food intake, and so food becomes so incredibly important and special. Much more than the actual lifeline that it is to all of us each day. So much more...

And yes, I am still overweight today. Yes, I would still like to be smaller and I still have a part of me that yearns to be that little girl again, but I know that I will never go down that path again. Today I have far healthier ways of finding that security and safety that I was so desperate for. I can talk to friends, take time out to relax when I need to wind down, I can listen to music, draw, read, or write—whatever is in my heart at that moment.

Plus I can now acknowledge that my body isn't *who* I am…it is the merely outside shell of the person I am inside, and although I would still prefer it to be a far more slender shell, it is more than good enough for me today. After all, why should I waste today yearning to be something I am not and that I most definitely won't magically become in the next twenty-four hours? I can work long-term towards being something that I want to be but I am only wasting my life if I spend today grieving for all that I'm not.

Besides, there is no such thing as being the 'right' weight or the 'right' size. There is never a magical number that you can hit and your life will be perfect. If life were that simple, then no one would ever have problems, would they?! We would all head off to the gym or the slimming classes when the going got tough! We would all reach our magic numbers in weeks and then never know another day of unhappiness for the rest of our lives—as long as the numbers never changed, that is. If only it were as simple as that…

I can't complain about how I live today though. For today my life feels, in the main part, like a beautiful, smooth and creamy chocolate gateau, rather than the awful vat of grey soup which engulfed me on a daily basis for many years. I can look straight at this gateau which sits beside me always and smile deep inside. I feel no fear, no compulsion, and no threat to my sanity, for I know that it is every part mine and always will be. I don't need to frantically reach out and grab handfuls of it until it is all gone, for fear of it being suddenly taken away from me. I can eat this gateau of mine slice by wonderful slice, live my life day by beautiful day, and enjoy the richness and texture of every mouthful and of each minute.

The fear has subsided.

The foundations have strengthened.

I have survived to tell the tale, and so will you.

Just one slice of gateau for me today, thank you…

******

Take My Hand, Little Anne

I can see you there.
Still hiding in the dark corners and still so afraid to come out.
But it's okay now.
It really is okay.
Nobody is going to hurt you and even if they try, then I am here to take care of you.
Together we will fight all the dragons and the demons and the little pictures in the darkness and we will win, I promise you.
You don't have to be afraid anymore.
Nobody is going to shout at you and tell you that you are bad.
Nobody is going to hit you.
Nobody is going to make you feel as if you shouldn't even be here.
I am going to take your hand, you see, and I am going to make it all okay.

You can eat now, you can make yourself warm, and you can feel snug and cosy and safe.
You don't have to hurt yourself anymore.
You don't have to feel that you deserve to be hurt.
You can look after yourself too, like all the other children do.
It's really going to be okay.

Do you trust me enough to take hold of my hand?
I can lead you out of the shadows and we can play in the light forever.
I will never let you go.
I will be beside you for always and eternity.

You will never have to be alone and scared again.
You will never be left alone to wonder what is happening, what bad thing is coming next.
I will show you that everything will always work out just as it is meant to be.
Take my hand, feel my strength.
Everything will be okay.

You don't have to be afraid to be you any more as you are more than enough.
Far more than enough.
You are special, you are unique, and you are here for a reason.
Together we will change our world.
Together we can make a difference.
But I need you to come out of the darkness and take hold of my hand.
Can you do that for me?

Just stretch out your fingers.
Reach out your arm.
There...it is safe; nobody is here but me.
I won't hurt you, I am here to love and protect you.
Just a little further then you can touch me.
There...
I can take hold of your hand now, doesn't that feel so much better?

We will come out of the shadows together, very slowly, and we will stand in the light.
Shade your eyes, you have been back there for so very long.
There is no need to tremble, there's nothing to fear.
I am here by your side, I am going nowhere.
Look up to the sunlight; let it warm up your face
See? You are starting to smile already...
It really is okay, isn't it?

Take my hand, Little Anne.
Walk beside me, walk with me, and trust me forever.
You will always be safe....
I promise you....